ACONCAGUA
a climbing guide

ACONCAGUA
a climbing guide

Second Edition

R. J. SECOR

THE
MOUNTAINEERS

Published by
The Mountaineers
1001 SW Klickitat Way, Suite 201
Seattle, Washington 98134

First edition 1994. Second edition: first printing 1999, second printing 2001, third printing 2002, fourth printing 2003, fifth printing 2004, sixth printing 2006, seventh printing 2009

Distributed in the United Kingdom by Cordee, www.cordee.co.uk

Manufactured in the United States of America

Edited by Uma Kukathas, Crystal Thomas
Maps by Dee Molenaar
All photographs by R. J. Secor unless otherwise noted
Cover design by Kristy L. Welch
Book design and layout by Kristy L. Welch
Cover photograph: *Aconcagua* © James W. Kay
Frontispiece: *Climbing the Normal Route, Aconcagua.* Photo by R. J. Secor

Library of Congress Cataloging-in-Publication Data
Secor, R. J.
    Aconcagua : a climbing guide / by R.J. Secor. — 2nd ed
    p. cm.
    Published simultaneously in Great Britain by Cordee.
    Includes bibliographical references (p. 116) and index.
    ISBN 0-89886-669-3 (pbk. : alk. paper)
    1. Mountaineering—Argentina—Aconcagua, Mount—Guidebooks. 2.
Aconcagua, Mount (Argentina)—Guidebooks. I. Title.
    GV199.44.A72 A2677 1999
    796.52'2'09826—dc21
                                                    99-6334
                                                    CIP

CONTENTS

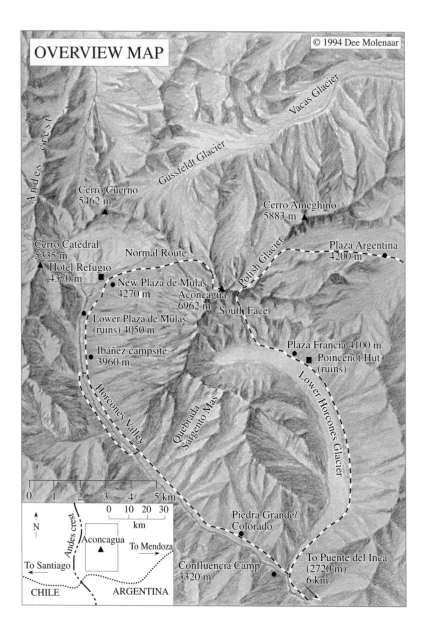

OVERVIEW MAP

© 1994 Dee Molenaar

Andes crest

Vacas Glacier

Güssfeldt Glacier

Cerro Cuerno
5462 m

Cerro Ameghino
5883 m

Cerro Catedral
5335 m
Hotel Refugio
4370 m

Normal Route

Polish Glacier

Plaza Argentina
4200 m

New Plaza de Mulas
4270 m

Aconcagua
6962 m

South Face

Lower Plaza de Mulas
(ruins) 4050 m

Plaza Francia 4100 m
Poincenot Hut
(ruins)

Ibáñez campsite
3960 m

Lower Horcones Glacier

Horcones Valley

Quebrada Sargento Mas

0 1 2 3 4 5 km

0 10 20 30
km

N

Andes crest

Aconcagua

To Mendoza

To Santiago

CHILE   ARGENTINA

Piedra Grande/
Colorado

Confluencia Camp
3320 m

To Puente del Inca
(2720 m)
6 km

Hiking up the Horcones Valley

ACKNOWLEDGMENTS

SECOND EDITION

I am grateful for the assistance given by Julie Rush, James Rice, Mark McKain, Jan Bongenaar, Eduardo Ibarra, Sergio A. Ciancia, Manuel C. Martín Sjoberg, Ricardo D. Román, Antonio Longás, Carlos Fernandez, Jorge Guardia, Gabriel Bairacliotti, Andres Garcia, and Fernando Grajales. I thank my climbing partner Alois Smrz, and Cory and Elena Hinds.

This book was edited by Uma Kukathas and production details were coordinated by Cindy Bohn, with the help of Crystal Thomas, Christine Ummel, and Kristy L. Welch.

R. J. Secor
Pasadena, California
January 1999

FIRST EDITION

This book is much stronger due in large part to the assistance I received from the following individuals:

Primary recognition should go to Cynthia Carey, a librarian at the Pasadena Public Library. I asked her to search some databases to find some oblique, aerial photographs of Aconcagua. This initial search was unsuccessful, but she kept the project in mind, and more than a year later she was instrumental in locating the photographs. This quest was assisted by Cheryl Sund of the U.S. Geological Survey Library in Denver, and I am grateful for the attention that April Goebel of the National Geographic Society gave to my request to search the society's archives.

I am also thankful for the assistance I received from the provincial government of Mendoza. Juan Carlos Vinassa, Professora Mirta Barosa, and Rubén Arnaldo Bielli of the Subsecretaria de Turismo were very helpful. Ricardo Haro, a ranger at the Parque Provincial Aconcagua, and Doug Paulson, a U.S. National Park Service ranger serving as a Peace Corps volunteer, spoke with me about the environmental problems that the park has experienced and the solutions that they have implemented.

Also of assistance were Maria de las Mercedes Ramirez de Nadal, Ramon Bustos, and Alfredo Berón of the Biblioteca de Sanmartiniano in the city of Mendoza.

Carlos Mercado, Maria Silvoni, Alberto Irisarri, and Alejandra Schegnfet of the Club Andinista Mendoza were invaluable; they not only allowed me access to the club's library, they also shared with me their private climbing notes. Others in Mendoza who were of assistance include: Yanina Geraci, Víctor Pettina, Luis Gabriel Ramon, Daniel Pizarro, David Ernesto Vela, Consuelo Quiroga, Oscar Escobeda, Andres Garcia, Cristina Oltra, Carlos Fernandez, Antonio Longás, Carlos Ruiz, Osvaldo Chirino, Jorge Crescitelli, and Daniel Alessio.

Also of help were Michael Chessler, Sigrid Hutto, Ralph Mackey, Jeff Thomas, Keith Mischke, Dave Nettle, John Bouchard, Evelio Echevarría, Stuart Ritchie, Chuck Armatys, Alex Lowe, Ryszard Kolakowski, Miguel Helft, Tom Taplin, and Mark Adrian. And I would be remiss if I didn't acknowledge my Aconcagua climbing partners: Rick Beatty, Kurt Wedberg, James Hilger, and Jack Miller.

And I want to thank the publishing staff of The Mountaineers, under the direction of Donna DeShazo, for their longtime support of my climbing guidebooks. Linda L. Robinson's professional editing made me look good. Helen Cherullo oversaw the production responsibilities, with the help of Marge Mueller, Rick May, Storm Yanicks, and additional editorial assistance from Christine Clifton-Thornton.

R. J. Secor
Pasadena, California
June 1994

INTRODUCTION

Aconcagua is one of the great mountains of the world, and it attracts mountaineers from all over the globe. Many North American climbers get their first glance of Aconcagua from the window of a jet aircraft as it makes its approach and descent for a landing at Santiago. This first impression is likely to be disappointing. Viewed from the northwest during the height of the austral summer, it appears to be one giant pile of scree. No glaciers or prominent rock walls can be seen. Those with a penchant for alpine scholarship may recall the words of the noted American writer and mountaineer, James Ramsey Ullman: "The reports of the various parties who have battled their way to its summit are unanimous in declaring that, from the point of view of climbing, it is one of the most unattractive mountains imaginable. In the alpine sense there are few, if any difficulties. There is little call for climbing skill or generalship. Yet its altitude is so great, its cold so bitter, its storms so frequent and savage, that the ascent ranks among the most grueling ordeals known to climbers. 'An intolerably monotonous slag-pile'; 'the dump-heap of South America'—these are merely two of the more printable epithets hurled at it by its battered and exhausted challengers."[1] Ullman wrote from his own experience; he made the first American ascent of Aconcagua in 1928.

The next sighting may be from the highway between Santiago and Mendoza. From this angle, the great South Face is visible, with its huge, vertical seracs and hanging glaciers, and at times it may be difficult to tell the difference between low-lying clouds and the lingering dust of avalanches. Climbers' reactions to this view range from enthusiasm to terror. A few days later the mountain may be seen from the Vacas Valley. From this angle part of the South Face may be seen. The difficult East Glacier is clearly visible, but most prominent of all is the Polish Glacier, rising and increasing in angle from right to left, where the summit ridge seems to touch the sky. Aconcagua doesn't show its best side to everyone.

Between White Rocks and the Independencia hut on the Normal Route

In my own view, Aconcagua is a paradoxical mountain. Its South Face has some of the most severe routes in the Andes, while the standard route along the Northwest Ridge features a well-worn path with shelters. Between these two extremes are the moderate Polish Glacier, the seldom-climbed Southwest Ridge, and the difficult East Glacier. Aconcagua is readily accessible from the highway between Mendoza and Santiago. But it is this easy access combined with the "walk-up" of the Normal Route that disguises the nature of the peak. The challenge of the mountain comes from high altitude and severe weather, and these two factors should never be underestimated during preparations for an ascent. There are other routes on the mountain that are within the capabilities of most climbers. I hope that this modest book will encourage climbers to consider attempting other routes on the high point of the Western Hemisphere, while tempering their enthusiasm with honest warnings about thin air, subzero temperatures, and high winds.

Another goal of this book is to encourage mountaineers to keep the mountain clean. Lightweight mountaineering expeditions are the current style, not only because these trips are easy to carry out, but also because it is easier to carry out the trash! The Aconcagua Provincial Park has done an excellent job of cleaning the mountain and its approach routes, and the park and the mountain should be in good shape for many years to come. But there is an ever-increasing number of climbers on Aconcagua each year, and it remains to be seen if a quota system will be established to limit climbers and their impacts. In another book, I wrote: "Let us not allow increased usage . . . to lead to environmental costs."[2] In the case of Aconcagua, I am going to rephrase this to say: Let us not allow environmental damage to limit the freedom that mountaineers now enjoy.

I expect that foreign mountaineers will take the time to see more of Argentina, and not limit their activities just to climbing mountains. One of the attractions of foreign travel is learning how other people live, to uncover their values, and to reflect upon one's own life and values. There is much more to the world than climbing mountains, but in my experience, mountaineering is one of the best ways to learn more about the world.

A NOTE ABOUT SAFETY

Safety is an important concern in all outdoor activities. No guidebook can alert you to every hazard or anticipate the limitations of every reader. Therefore, the descriptions of roads, trails, routes, and natural features in this book are not representations that a particular place or excursion will be safe for your party. When you follow any of the routes described in this book, you assume responsibility for your own safety. Under normal conditions, such excursions require the usual attention to traffic, road and trail conditions, weather, terrain, the capabilities of your party, and other factors. Keeping informed on current conditions and exercising common sense are the keys to a safe, enjoyable outing.

Political conditions may add to the risks of travel in South America in ways that this book cannot predict. When you travel, you assume this risk, and should keep informed of political developments that may make safe travel difficult or impossible.

The Mountaineers

Chapter One
HISTORY

The Ayamará Indians, living in today's Province of Mendoza, named the mountain *Kon-Kawa,* or Snowy Mountain, while the Chilean Indians, the Araucanos, named the river on the western side of the Andean crest *Aconca-Hue,* or "It comes from the other side." The Inca empire eventually reached the central Andes, where they called the mountain *Ancocahuac,* made up of the Quechua words *anco* (white) and *cahuac* (sentinel). There is no definitive proof that the Incas actually climbed to the summit of the White Sentinel, but there is considerable evidence that the ancient Incas climbed very high on the mountain. Signs of Inca ascents have been found on summits throughout the Andes, thus far the highest atop Llullaillaco, a 6721-m (22,051-ft) mountain astride the Chilean-Argentine border in the Puna de Atacama region. On Aconcagua, the skeleton of a guanaco (a wild relative of the llama) was found in 1947 along the ridge connecting the North and South Summits. It seems doubtful that a guanaco would climb that high on the mountain on its own, and several archaeologists have visited the Cresta del Guanaco (Guanaco Crest) looking for Inca sites, with no definitive discoveries along this ridge. But the most significant find happened in 1985 with the discovery of a mummy (preserved by cold, dry air, not by embalming) at the 5200-m (17,060-ft) level along the southwest ridge of Cerro Piramidal, a 6009-m (19,714-ft) peak along Aconcagua's Southwest Ridge. It is widely thought that there are other undiscovered archaeological sites on Aconcagua, and those with information should contact Centro de Investigaciones Arqueológicas de Alta Montaña, República del Líbano 2621, Correo de Capitán Lazo, 5423 San Juan, Argentina. It should be stressed that *nothing should be taken or moved* from a known or suspected archaeological site. This is not only the law in Argentina, but common sense as well. I find it quite intriguing that the ancient Incas

Nieve Penitentes

were the first to have made ascents of mountains over 6000 m (19,685 ft), and it would be a great loss to humankind if this evidence is disturbed before it can be investigated.[3]

The first significant European exploration of the Central Andes took place in 1817, when General José de San Martín crossed the range to liberate Chile from the Spanish. San Martín spent three years preparing the "Army of the Andes" and proposed attacking the Spanish at Santiago and Valparaiso overland from the passes surrounding Mercedario, Aconcagua, and Tupungato. This army consisted of 5,300 soldiers, 10,600 mules, and 1,600 horses; they dragged their artillery over 4000-m (13,120-ft) passes, hindered considerably by scree and snowfields, to surprise the Spanish, who expected any invasion to come from the sea. But this victory did not come without great cost—the bodies of a total 6,000 mules and 1,000 horses marked their routes across the Andes.

In 1832, Charles Darwin noted the dominant presence of Aconcagua while crossing the Andes during a journey ashore on the voyage of the *Beagle*. But the first serious European attempt on the mountain was made in 1883 by Paul Güssfeldt, one of the most accomplished German alpinists of the late nineteenth century.

Güssfeldt approached Aconcagua from Santiago, and recruited muleteers by perpetuating the myth that there was buried treasure on the mountain. He crossed the Andean crest to the northwest of Aconcagua, and made the final approach by ascending the Río Volcán. Güssfeldt made two bold attempts to reach the summit from the head of this river. He was more successful in his first attempt, traversing the Northwest Ridge to reach an altitude of 6560 m (21,522 ft, near where the Independencia hut is located today). While this expedition was unsuccessful, it was a remarkable one, considering the difficulties of the approach and the poor equipment available at that time, and it was the first to reconnoiter what was to become the Normal Route.

The first ascent of the Normal Route took place during 1896–1897 by an expedition under the leadership of Edward FitzGerald from England. FitzGerald's account of the expedition, *The Highest Andes,* is a classic work of mountaineering literature, in a league with Edward Whymper's *Travels Amongst the Great Andes of Ecuador*. With FitzGerald

was another English climber, Stuart Vines, and some Swiss and Italian porters under the direction of the renowned Swiss Guide, Matthias Zurbriggen. FitzGerald's first problem was determining the best approach to the mountain. He was aware of Güssfeldt's exploration, but believed that a better approach would be from the south, where a rudimentary road had been constructed between Santiago and Mendoza. They first ascended the Río de Vacas, and concluded that the eastern side of the mountain was not feasible, followed by the Lower Horcones Valley, which led them to the precipitous South Face. They then returned to the main Horcones Valley, and ascended it to its head. While today's Normal Route has a reputation for being no more than a walk, FitzGerald's expedition had to lay siege to Aconcagua. A total of five attempts over six weeks were needed before Matthias Zurbriggen arrived on the summit, alone, on January 14, 1897. Over the following month FitzGerald, Vines, and Nicola Lanti (one of their Italian porters) continued the siege, with Vines and Lanti reaching the summit on February 13. It is regrettable that FitzGerald was unable to climb to the top, due to recurrent bouts of altitude sickness. He was the originator and leader of the expedition, and his judgment, courage, and sense of humor were its anchor. After Aconcagua, the expedition moved to the south, and Vines and Zurbriggen made the first ascent of Tupungato (6550 m; 21,490 ft).

The next phase of exploratory mountaineering on Aconcagua was made in 1934 by a Polish expedition. Prior to the ascent of Aconcagua, the Poles had made the first ascent of Mercedario, a 6770-m (22,211-ft) mountain to the north.

The six-man party ascended the Vacas and Relinchos Valleys to the base of the east side of Aconcagua. The entire expedition started up the mountain on March 5, and made their first camp at 5500 m (18,044 ft). The next day they continued up to the prominent cliff that marks the northeast side of the mountain and camped at its base at 5900 m (19,357 ft). They found a route around the cliff the next day and climbed onto the glacier to continue up to their high camp at 6300 m (20,670 ft). Their ascent was marked to this point by bitterly cold temperatures with high winds. On March 8, Adam Karpinski and Voytek Dorwaski attempted to climb to the summit, but the conditions remained bad, and they were

forced to return to the site of their second camp. The wind lessened the next day, although the cold was still intense, and Stefan Daszyinski, Konstanty Narkievitcz-Jodko, Stefan Osiecki, and Wictor Ostrowski made another attempt. After 8 hours of strenuous climbing they reached the summit, making the first ascent of what would later be named the Polish Glacier. This strong party was from the High Tatras region of Poland, now famous for producing the leading Himalayan climbers of today, and the first ascent of the Polish Glacier was accomplished in alpine style, a climb far ahead of its time.

In 1948 a Swiss climber, Federico Marmillod, ascended the Normal Route. A resident of Argentina, he had spent the previous fifteen years exploring the Andes and had understandably become bored with the "desert" nature of the Central Andes. During the descent, he thought back to the fine climbs he had made in the Alps, and began to think of the possibilities for such routes in this region. This line of thinking led him to look at the Southwest Ridge of Aconcagua. In February of 1952, Marmillod, his wife Dorly, and Argentine Miguel Ruedin were ready to make an attempt, but fresh snow and bad weather forced them to take consolation in climbing the Normal Route instead. The next month Marmillod joined a French expedition to Aconcagua. This expedition had just made the first ascent of FitzRoy in Patagonia, and they were keen on attempting the South Face of Aconcagua. A brief glance at the South Face from the Lower Horcones Valley convinced the French climbers that this route was too much for them at that time, so instead they climbed the Normal Route. In this party was the French expedition's Argentine liaison officer, Lieutenant Francisco Ibáñez, and he and Marmillod made a quick reconnaissance of the approach to the Southwest Ridge and agreed to attempt it the next year.

Miguel Ruedin was unable to join them due to work commitments, and his place was taken by Fernando Grajales. He and Ibáñez had just climbed the Normal Route (this was Ibáñez's fifth ascent of this route), and they met the Marmillods at Plaza de Mulas in mid-January of 1953. The Marmillods had acclimatized by climbing Mirador and México, two 5000-m peaks to the south of Aconcagua, which also gave them the opportunity to scout the upper part of the route from a distance. Using

Aconcagua

mules, the party of four headed southeast from Plaza de Mulas, traversing across the scree slopes that mark the lower portion of the West Face of Aconcagua. Despite the preparation of a rough trail in the preceding days, the route proved to be too difficult for the mules, and the climbers were obliged to drop their loads at approximately 6000 m (19,684 ft), which became the party's first campsite.

This part of the mountain was blocked by a large, long cliff that had no apparent weakness. They spent the next day searching for a break in the cliff. At first they attempted a short, steep chute, but decided against it because they thought that they might need to save their strength for difficulties higher on the route. On January 20 they left this camp, with a Zdarsky bivouac sack for four in addition to their own air mattresses and sleeping bags. They traversed across the West Face beneath the line of cliffs until they found a deep couloir that permitted them to overcome this initial obstacle. Then they moved to the right and attempted to gain the crest of the Southwest Ridge, but found their way blocked by massive towers of crumbly rock. Instead, they had to traverse back to

the left and down to the base of a huge couloir, where they found a good bivouac site under an overhanging rock; this site was only 200 meters (656 feet) above their previous camp! Their route thus far had assumed a huge, hair-pinned shape. The next day they continued up the huge couloir, which in places consisted of bare ice between vertical walls, to their next bivouac at 6400 m (20,997 ft). That night the weather broke, and snow gradually sifted into their bivouac sack. The storm lasted through the next day, slowly diminishing in intensity to a clear sunset. They left this bivouac in the morning of January 23, and climbed the upper part of the West Face to the crest of the Southwest Ridge. They were rewarded with a clear sky, along with a magnificent view of the South Face of Aconcagua and the entire Central Andes, from Tupungato to the south to Mercedario to the north, with the Pacific Ocean to the west. They traversed the South Summit, and descended the Normal Route, pleased with their success.

The next challenge was the South Face of Aconcagua. This is a huge face, almost 3000 m (10,000 ft) high, defended by bands of loose rock, ice cliffs, and huge avalanches. It is no exaggeration to say that this face is comparable to two Eigers, one stacked on top of the other. In January 1954 a French expedition under the leadership of René Ferlet with Guy Poulet, Robert Pagarot, Edmond Denis, Pierre Lasueur, Lucien Berardini, and Andrien Dagory established a base camp at 4500 m (14,764 ft) along the Lower Horcones Glacier; the base could not be established directly beneath the South Face, due to the threat of avalanches. The expedition started up the logical route on this face, the central rib, but soon found vertical cliffs of rotten rock and were obliged to fix approximately 400 meters (1,300 feet) of fixed rope. This led them to the base of a rock band beneath the main hanging glacier on the face. The rock band was overcome by means of a difficult vertical chimney that took 7 hours to lead. In addition to the threat of avalanches from the hanging glacier, Aconcagua's famous winds plagued the climbers throughout the climb.

After one month of effort, all of the climbers (except for Ferlet, who had descended after an attack of sciatica) gathered at their fifth camp at 6400 m (21,000 ft) and began the final assault. They were soon faced with time-consuming direct-aid climbing and were forced to bivouac

high on the face. The party finally reached the summit at 8:00 P.M. the following evening. They descended the Normal Route in darkness and had difficulty locating the General Perón shelter (now known as the Independencia hut). All but two found the shelter; fortunately the two missing climbers were found by some Chilean climbers and an Argentine army patrol that night. All of the descending French climbers had deep frostbite, which they aggravated with vigorous massage and by beating their frozen toes and fingers with ropes! They resumed their painful descent the following morning and were evacuated to Mendoza, where they spent many weeks recovering from their severe frostbite and subsequent amputations.

Each of Aconcagua's major sides had been climbed by the mid-1950s, and over the following years more routes and variations were pioneered. The next historical phase shifted from exploration to management. The Argentine army controlled the mountain for many years, and while obtaining permission from the army to climb Aconcagua was a stringent procedure, many climbers are nostalgic about this period, because the army provided mules to mountaineering expeditions for free! This practice came to an end in 1980 (the sudden shift to private enterprise resulted in sky-high mule rates, which remain to this day), and Argentina's military rule ended in 1983, a major event in Argentine history. During the same year the Province of Mendoza created the Aconcagua Provincial Park, declaring it a protected natural area.

Aconcagua became a major destination for mountaineers from all over the world in the 1980s. During the 1983–1984 season, 346 climbers attempted the mountain. Ten years later, this number had increased to well over 2,000 climbers in one season. The park's managers gradually began measures to clean and maintain the mountain for future generations of climbers. More than eight metric tons of rubbish was removed from the Horcones Valley in 1990, and carry-it-in/carry-it-out rules were strictly enforced by park rangers. But the number of climbers who attempt Aconcagua continues to grow each year, and Aconcagua's last great problem is not in the realm of new routes, but in the practice of clean climbing. From this perspective, all mountaineers have the potential to make a significant contribution to the history of Aconcagua.

HOW HIGH IS ACONCAGUA?

The altitude of Aconcagua seems to be in continual dispute, as is the altitude of its rival for the high point of South America, Ojos del Salado. These questions have existed for forty years, fueled by rumor, gossip, hearsay, and speculation, rather than cold and sterile facts.

Ojos del Salado is located along the Chilean–Argentine border in the Puna de Atacama, approximately 640 kilometers (400 miles) north of Aconcagua. It was first climbed in 1937 by J. Wojsznis and J. A. Szczepanski, two members of a Polish expedition. But it entered the alpine limelight in 1955 after a press report mistakenly declared "the first ascent of the highest mountain in the western hemisphere, Ojos del Salado, 7100 m (23,294 ft)." Subsequent investigations revealed that an Argentine expedition from Tucumán mistakenly believed that they had made the first ascent of Ojos del Salado, while in fact they had climbed an unnamed and unclimbed mountain 10 to 13 kilometers (6 to 8 miles) south of, and about 240 meters (800 feet) lower than Ojos del Salado. The expedition also stated that it was possible that Ojos del Salado was higher than Aconcagua. Unfortunately, the media interpreted this blunder and wishful thinking as fact. Spurred by this report, a Chilean expedition climbed the real Ojos del Salado the following year and claimed an altitude of 7084 m (23,241 ft). The press again reported this to be an exact altitude, but this figure was obtained by reading an aneroid altimeter, a notoriously inaccurate method of determining altitude.

In the midst of this speculation the American Alpine Club fielded an expedition to Ojos del Salado during the austral winter of 1956. The party was under the leadership of H. Adams Carter, and included Anne Carter, Bob Bates, Gail Bates, John Wylde, and Peter Weaver as the chief surveyor. With the support of the Chilean army, the party approached Ojos del Salado from the northwest and conducted a trigonometric survey of the mountain. They determined that Ojos del Salado was 6885.5 m (22,590 ft) above sea level, with a probable error of plus or minus three meters.[4]

The altitude of Aconcagua was initially surveyed by the Argentine Instituto Geográfico Militar (Military Geographic Institute) in the 1920s during a survey of the trans-Andean railway between Santiago and Mendoza. From this trigonometric survey, the altitude of Aconcagua was

determined to be 7021 m (23,035 ft), a figure that continues to appear with distressing regularity. In 1956, during the height of the debate over Aconcagua versus Ojos del Salado, Eduardo E. Baglietto of the University of Buenos Aires decided to determine the exact altitude of Aconcagua during a geodetic survey of the Central Andes. With the help of his colleagues and graduate students from the university and the Argentine army, it was determined that Aconcagua had an altitude of 6959.7 m (22,834 ft), with a probable error of plus or minus one meter.[5]

In the 1980s, the placement of Global Positioning System (GPS) satellites eased the tedious work involved in conducting trigonometric surveys. Also, the accuracy of such surveys can be enhanced by placing a GPS receiver at an unknown elevation site (such as a mountain summit) along with several other receivers placed at known altitude sites (such as benchmarks). Francesco Santon, from the University of Padua in Italy, used GPS technology to survey both Aconcagua and Ojos del Salado in 1989 with the help of his colleagues from Padua, the Argentine Institute of Glaciology and Nivology, and Argentine mountaineers. Ojos del Salado was determined to be 6900 m (22,637 ft), and Aconcagua was 6962 m (22,841 ft) above sea level, with a possible error of plus or minus five meters.[6]

Chapter Two
PREPARATIONS

THE TEAM

At present, an expedition does not need a minimum number of climbers to obtain permission to climb Aconcagua. (Or perhaps I should rephrase this to say that an expedition needs at least one member to qualify for a permit!) Nor does the team need to have a minimum amount of experience to obtain a permit. But in the real world, climbing a peak that almost touches 7000 m (23,000 ft) requires as much high altitude experience as possible. In my own view, I would estimate that the minimum amount of experience needed to attempt Aconcagua by either the Normal Route or the Polish Glacier would be at least three years of general mountaineering experience climbing 3000- to 4000-m (10,000- to 13,000-ft) peaks in all seasons, with some exposure to higher altitudes (such as climbing Mexico's volcanoes), and considerable study of the problems of climbing at high altitude in the cold.

Aconcagua has been soloed (even some routes on the South Face have been soloed!) and, conversely, some remarkably large expeditions (more than twenty members) have had great success on the mountain. Speaking generally, each extra expedition member adds to the party's safety, but it seems that each extra person exponentially increases the amount of group equipment carried, and this subtracts from the team's general efficiency.

Perhaps the best size for a party would be from a minimum of four to a maximum of eight climbers to make the team as self-sufficient as possible. But as British mountaineer Alan Rouse once said, "From my personal experience I have concluded that the most successful expeditions are those which split into pairs of climbers,"[7] and to this I would add that this tactic should preferably be planned before the expedition. Two is a natural size for a climbing and camping team, and it is easy for the pair to decide on what equipment they will carry; this cuts down on the total amount of group equipment carried. Pairs reduce the pressure

quickly, and it offers door-to-door service between Santiago and Mendoza, even meeting the party at the airport with a reservation. The road from Santiago to Mendoza passes through the Chilean communities of Colina and Los Andes, and a brief stop for last-minute purchases may be arranged with the collective taxi driver. This is an attractive option, as prices are generally less in Chile than in Argentina, but these purchases should be made in Chilean pesos. And after the climb, it is very easy to negotiate one's way onto an express bus or collective taxi to Santiago at the Argentine customs station just west of Puente del Inca.

SCHEDULES

Aconcagua has been climbed in less than 5 hours via the Normal Route from Plaza de Mulas. But most mortal climbers do (and should) spend a bit more time climbing the mountain.

The Normal Route on Aconcagua can be climbed in three weeks, round trip from North America. This includes a day of travel to South America, a day of travel to Mendoza, one day in Mendoza, a day of travel to Puente del Inca, and two days to approach the standard base camp, Plaza de Mulas. Up to 11 days are available to climb the mountain with this schedule (aside from the speed demons mentioned above, some parties have taken as few as 3 days from Plaza de Mulas to reach the summit, while others needed as many as 14 days), with 4 days to descend to Puente de Inca and return to North America.

The other popular route is the Polish Glacier, which can be climbed in four weeks round trip from North America. The approach from Punta de Vacas to Plaza Argentina (the base camp for the Polish Glacier) is longer than the approach to Plaza de Mulas from Puente del Inca, and an extra day is usually needed by many parties. So plan on arriving at Plaza Argentina on the seventh day after leaving North America. Up to 15 days are available to climb the Polish Glacier with this schedule, with 6 more days to return to North America.

But these are only guidelines. I know of an expedition to the Polish Glacier that managed to hike in to Plaza Argentina in only 2 days, climbed the mountain over a period of 11 days from base camp, and took another 2 days to return to Punta de Vacas. A total of three weeks from North America was taken for this climb.

Los Penitentes Ski Area

Of course, it should be noted that in 1898 Sir Martin Conway (at the age of 42) and Antoine Maquignaz came very close to the summit of Aconcagua (Conway estimated that their high point was 100 feet below, and 100 yards from the summit). This party approached the mountain with mules, and the attempt was accomplished in five and a half days, round trip from Puente del Inca.[8]

A noteworthy ascent of the Normal Route took place in 1980 by William and Mireille Marks. Climbs of Aconcagua in the early 1980s were hampered by the excessive problems with obtaining permission

from the authorities. On Sunday, February 10, the Marks finally gained permission to climb, and left Puente del Inca to reach the summit on Friday the 15th. They returned to the trailhead on the following Sunday, February 17. The approach was accomplished without the aid of mules, and as William Marks later wrote: "Not bad for my wife and me, both over fifty years old."[9]

Most North American parties fly to South America on a Saturday, and start their approach to base camp on the following Wednesday. This results in crowded lodgings at Puente del Inca and Los Penitentes on Tuesday nights, great demand for mules on Wednesday, and a lot of company during the approach hike over Thursday, Friday, and Saturday. It may be better to avoid the subsequent rush by leaving North America on a Monday or Tuesday. Also, many expeditions plan to go for the summit a few days after the full moon, to help illuminate the predawn start.

MENDOZA

One of the attractions of a trip to Aconcagua is visiting the charming city of Mendoza (740 m, 2,428 ft; 32° 50'S, 68° 45'W). Many North Americans travel to Mendoza with the misperception that it has the same level of development as a similar-sized city in a less-developed country, and are surprised to find a clean, modern city, comparable to one in Europe. It is Argentina's fourth largest city, with a population of one million (including surrounding suburbs). It is a bustling commercial, oil-processing, wine-producing, and fruit-farming center. Compared with the rest of the arid pampas, it is an oasis with many parks, sidewalk cafes, lots of shade trees, delicious Argentine beef, and fine, yet inexpensive, wines. The ambiance is more casual than in other Argentine cities, and during hot summer days T-shirts, shorts, and sandals are commonly seen. There are very few incidents of violent crime, but it is always a good idea to remain vigilant, no matter where one is traveling. In my experience, the biggest dangers of walking at night are tripping on cracked sidewalks and falling into one of the huge gutters that line the streets. This probably says more about me than the city of Mendoza!

Foreign climbers may want to visit the local alpine club, the Club Andinista Mendoza (don't confuse this with the Club Andino Mendoza,

an athletic club). The club is located at Beltrán 357, in Guaymallén, a suburb to the east of central Mendoza. The telephone number is 54-261-425-1281. It is open Monday through Friday from 8:30 P.M. to 10:30 P.M. and features aerial photographs of Aconcagua and other memorabilia from Argentine mountain ascents from around the world. The club membership has the most up-to-date information on Aconcagua, but its main area of interest is the Cordon del Plata, a range of 5000-m (16,404-ft) peaks that is 65 kilometers (40 miles) to the southeast of Aconcagua, near the Vallecitos ski area. The Club Andinista Mendoza maintains some huts and refuges in this area, and the members can be found there every weekend throughout the year. The mailing address is Club Andinista Mendoza, C.C. 400, 5500 Mendoza, Argentina.

Mountaineering equipment is very expensive in Argentina, with typical retail prices almost three times more than the usual North American price. The Club Andinista Mendoza would be a good place to sell climbing equipment after an expedition.

There are many places to stay in Mendoza, from four-star hotels to youth hostels, and many North American climbers stay at the Hotel Nutibara, located at Mitre 867, 5500 Mendoza, Argentina (telephone: 54-261-429-5428, located at the corner of Mitre and Montevideo. It is owned by an Argentine climber, and the helpful (and tolerant) staff is used to dealing with the peculiar demands that *andinistas* have while preparing for a big climb. There is a large sundeck and a recreation room, and it is common to see climbers sorting gear in these places, with knapsacks, duffels, and shopping bags strewn about. This hotel also features a swimming pool, air conditioning, and a bar. Other hotels that seem to be popular with climbers are the four-star Hotel Aconcagua at San Lorenzo 545, 5500 Mendoza (telephone: 54-261-420-4499; fax: 54-261-420-2083; email: aconcaguahotel@infovia.com.ar), the Hotel Balbi at Las Heras 340, 5500 Mendoza (telephone: 54-261-423-3500; fax: 54-261-438-0626), Hotel Murano at Las Heras 558, 5500 Mendoza (telephone: 54-261-425-4482), Hotel Horcones at Las Heras 145, 5500 Mendoza (telephone: 54-261-428-2052; fax: 54-261-425-0045), and Hotel Rincon Vasco at Las Heras 590, 5500 Mendoza (telephone: 54-261-423-3033). Budget accomodations include Hospedaje Lucense at Chile 759, 5500 Mendoza (telephone: 54-261-423-9088), and a youth hostel at Campo Base, Mitre 946, 5500 Mendoza (tele-

Mendoza

phone: 54-261-429-0707; email: info@campo-base.com.ar).

Argentines eat very well, and this will become readily apparent upon visiting any restaurant in Mendoza. (The only time I became ill from Argentine food and water was after eating *too much* food!) A typical Argentine dish is *el bife a caballo,* which literally translates into "steak on horseback." In reality, this is one or two fried eggs placed atop a large beef steak, and is typically served with *papas fritas* (French fries). The meal isn't complete without wine, and all Mendoza restaurants offer tourists a bottle of wine (*vino turista*) for U.S. $2.50. A popular restaurant among North American climbers is El Meson Español at Montevideo 244. While this restaurant is a little expensive, its main attraction is the talented pianist, Charlie "El Lucho" Fernandez, who speaks fluent, idiomatic English. He does a remarkable job of keeping track of the comings and goings of foreign *andinistas,* and his skill at the keyboard guarantees a memorable night on the town in Mendoza.

Vegetarians may tire of eating only *papas fritas.* For variety, Asia, at San Martín 821, serves Argentine and Chinese cuisine buffet style.

As in other Latin American countries, there is an afternoon *siesta.*

Stores, shops, and money exchange houses are typically open from 8:30 A.M. to 12:30 P.M. and from 4:30 P.M. to 8:30 P.M. Banks are open from 8:00 A.M. to 1:00 P.M. A big lunch is served from 1:00 P.M. to 3:00 P.M., and an equally large dinner is served from 9:00 P.M. to 11:00 P.M. Argentina's telephone country code is 54, and Mendoza's area code is 261. One must dial a "0" before the area code when calling long distance within Argentina.

Argentine national holidays are on January 1, Good Friday, Easter, May 1, May 25, June 10, June 20, July 9, August 17, October 12, and December 25. In addition, Mendoza provincial holidays are on January 18, July 25, and September 8. Chilean national holidays are on January 1, Good Friday, Easter, May 1, May 21, August 15, September 11, September 18, September 19, October 12, November 1, December 8, and December 25.

CLIMBING PERMITS AND OUTFITTERS

Obtaining a climbing permit (permiso de ascenso) for Aconcagua is a relatively simple process. Each individual can obtain his or her climbing permit from the Dirección de Bosques y Parques Provicinciales (Department of Provincial Forests and Parks), Province of Mendoza. This office is located in the city of Mendoza, just south of the main entrance of General San Martín Park, where Libertador and Emilio Civit meet. The office is open Monday through Friday from 8:00 A.M. to 6:00 P.M. and on Saturdays, Sundays, and holidays from 9:00 A.M. to 1:00 P.M. (Permits are not available on Christmas or New Year's Day.)

All climbers must obtain their climbing permits in person at the office, and they should be ready to complete the applications listing their full legal name, address, blood type, sex, citizenship, passport number, age, role on the expedition, medical and rescue insurance policy numbers (if covered), emergency notification, proposed base camp site, and planned routes of ascent and descent. (By the way, the permit application is in English and Spanish). This permit is valid for 20 days after entering the park. The permit fee varies from a low of US$100 during the slow seasons (November 15–30 and February 21–March 15) to a high of US$300 during the busy season (December 15–January 31) and during the austral winter (May 1–November 14). The fee is US$200

December 1–14 and February 1–20, but citizens of Argentina receive a fifty percent discount during this period. (Argentines also receive a fifty percent discount in the early winter from March 16–April 30; foreigners pay US$200 between these dates.

It is necessary to show the permit to the park rangers based at the Horcones Valley control station (the approach for the Normal Route) or at the La Leña control station along the Río de las Vacas (the Polish Glacier approach), and to the park rangers based at Plaza de Mulas (the Normal Route base camp) or Plaza Argentina (the Polish Glacier base camp). The rangers will take a copy of your permit, and in turn outline the park regulations: no wood campfires, firearms, or hunting; don't destroy the plants or remove fossils or archeological artifacts; camp only in authorized sites (during the approach); and pack out all rubbish generated by the party. The ranger will issue each party a numbered trash bag and note the number on each member's permit. Upon completion of the climb, a park ranger signs each individual's permit, verifying that the expedition's rubbish was packed out. In most cases this is done at Plaza de Mulas or Plaza Argentina, and the trash bag will be packed out by the party's muleteer. Or the party can pack it out themselves to either the La Leña or Horcones Valley control stations. Those who attempt to exit the park

Checking the permit at Horcones Ranger Station

without a signed permit or full trash bag will be cited and forced to pay a hefty fine; this regulation has been strictly enforced in recent years! In addition to the climbing permit, a trekking permit is also available. The fee for a 3-day trekking permit varies from US$20 to US$30, a 7-day trekking permit from $30 to $50, depending on the season and whether the applicant is a citizen of Argentina or of another country. Be sure to ask for and obtain the correct permit!

There are also outfitters in Mendoza that will make the permit process even easier, for a fee. Besides being aware of the latest permit requirements, they can also meet you at the airport, take you to your hotel where they have made advance reservations for you, go shopping for supplies, provide ground transportation to the trailhead, make arrangements for mules to carry the party's gear to base camp, provide meals at base camp, guard equipment left at base camp, and, in general, facilitate the endeavor. Using an outfitter to climb Aconcagua is not absolutely necessary (unlike climbs in Pakistan or Nepal where the outfitter is known as a "trekking agent"), but I would consider hiring an agent if I had a large group (six or more), didn't speak any Spanish, and wanted to save a day of time. A list of licensed outfitters, muleteers, and mountain guides, with addresses, telephone numbers, and fax numbers, is provided in Appendix D.

EQUIPMENT

The personal and group equipment needed for an expedition to Aconcagua is more or less the same as would be needed for a winter climb of a 3000- to 4000-m (10,000- to 13,000-ft) peak in the continental United States, with the possible exception of skis or snowshoes.

The most important item of personal equipment is cold-weather double mountaineering boots. Most climbers would agree with this statement, but they only take it as far as purchasing a stock pair of these boots off of the shelf (or by mail order) from a mountain shop. Most experienced high-altitude climbers have modified their stock boots to make them warmer and lighter. These "hot rods" can be as simple as purchasing a pair of oversized boots (one and a half to two American sizes larger than normal street size) and replacing the stock insoles with insoles from a pair of running shoes, or as complicated as a complete

Tents on exposed sites should have extra guy lines for security against high winds. This camp is at 6100 m (20,012 ft) on the Polish Glacier Route.

overhaul, requiring the services of a professional cobbler.

For example, I have had bad luck with stock inner-boots. The closed-cell foam in the inner-boots expanded at altitude. Although I had over-sized boots, the inner-boots expanded so much at 6000 m (20,000 ft) that it felt as if I was wearing a pair of iron maidens on my feet! At that time I was able to jury-rig another pair of inner-boots by cutting and gluing a foam pad to fit my feet, but on my next expedition I substituted a pair of felt shoe-pac liners for the stock inner-boots, with excellent results. The liners were warm and comfortable, the high-tech felt wicked moisture away from and reflected heat back onto my feet, they dried every night in my sleeping bag, and I started each day with warm feet. What's more, these liners are much less expensive than stock inner-boots, and they

are much lighter. The stock inner-boots weigh 680 grams (one and a half pounds); the liners weigh only 227 grams (half a pound)! And I know a climber who built his own inner boots out of closed-cell foam, shaving key locations for the perfect fit while adding insulation in other spots. The outer plastic shells were modified by a cobbler, who replaced the stiff plastic cuff with a flexible one to improve technique, ripped off the sole and replaced it with a lighter version, and added a built-in supergaiter. The stock version of these boots weighed 2778 grams (6 pounds, 2 ounces) while the hot rod weighed 2552 grams (5 pounds, 10 ounces)! The 226 grams (8 ounces) saved may not sound like much, but at altitude every ounce (28.35 grams) counts, and, physiologically, every pound (0.45 kilogram) on the feet is equivalent to five pounds (2.25 kilograms) on the back. So this amounts to a significant weight savings with a dramatic increase in warmth.

Speaking generally, Aconcagua has more rock than snow, and overboots are usually inconvenient. Supergaiters, which leave the sole of the boot exposed, are preferred for extra insulation over the feet.

Many climbers prefer a synthetic, wicking sock next to the foot, followed by a vapor barrier (a waterproof layer, anything from a simple plastic bag to a sock made of coated nylon), topped by a thick, heavy sock. Synthetic socks dry much more quickly than wool, but I have found wool socks to be more comfortable and warmer. My sock system consists of a wool/synthetic-blend liner sock, followed by a medium-weight wool sock, and finally a thick wool sock; I only add a vapor barrier when my feet are especially cold. Make sure that all of your sock layers don't fit tightly on your feet while wearing your oversized boots. A snug fit can lead to frostbite!

The key to clothing is the layering system. Layers can be added or discarded with temperature fluctuations. The first layer is some type of synthetic underwear that wicks moisture away from the skin and dries quickly. This is followed by two or more insulating layers, also preferably of synthetic pile, and a windproof outer layer. This system applies not only to the torso but also to the extremities. It is not uncommon to have a total of three layers on the legs, hands, and head, and perhaps as many as five layers on the torso. The last (perhaps ultimate) layer is a down or synthetic insulated jacket with a hood. This is seldom worn

while climbing, but is most appreciated during meals, in the pre-dawn hours of cold summit days, and perhaps during a bivouac. Make sure that all of the layers are sized so that they fit over each other without binding. And one cannot have too many pockets!

Most parties that have thermometers typically report low temperatures from –20 to –30 degrees C (–4 to –22 degrees F) at their high camps (the lowest temperature I have recorded on Aconcagua was –26 degrees C or –15 degrees F). So it follows that a sleeping bag rated for these temperatures would be needed, unless you know from experience that you could get away with something more lightweight. For example, I have had good luck with a light sleeping bag rated to –7 degrees C (+ 20 degrees F). I have used this bag not only on Aconcagua, but in some other cold, high places, and to be honest, many times I have had to wear an insulated jacket and add hot water bottles to remain comfortable throughout the night. But I rationalize using this bag because its light weight is a powerful incentive to eat and drink plenty, which is the ultimate source of warmth.[10] My sleeping system also includes two ten-millimeter (three-eighths-inch) closed-cell foam pads; I double the insulation underneath my torso and use my empty knapsack for additional padding under my legs.

Internal frame knapsacks are preferred by most climbers, due to their comfortable, close fit and low bulk. A minimum capacity would be approximately 70 liters (4400 cubic inches). External frame packs can also be used, but their bulk can interfere with balance while climbing, and they are inconvenient to strap onto a mule.

While the Normal Route on Aconcagua is little more than a trail, an ice axe and crampons should still be taken, at least as far as Plaza de Mulas, the base camp. The scree slopes on the upper part of the mountain can be covered by fields of snow and ice. And full crevasse rescue equipment should be carried while attempting the Polish Glacier.

One of the legends of Aconcagua is the *viento blanco,* or white wind. High winds are part of the experience of climbing the mountain. Winds in excess of 240 kilometers per hour (150 miles per hour) have been reported, and bombproof expedition-quality tents are mandatory items of equipment. Dome tents are the most popular, followed closely by hooped Quonset hut tents. A few climbers add shock.or bungee cords to

the tent guylines to help relieve the stress of high winds on these vulnerable structures.

The most important items of group equipment are the stoves. Stoves are used to melt snow for water, and the failure of a stove can be the failure of an expedition. Stoves should be light, compact, robust, and easy to maintain in the field. But the most important factor is experience with a stove's fickle personality under varied conditions with rigorous use. In this way, appropriate spare parts and tools can be brought on the expedition, along with the knowledge to keep the stoves running under all circumstances. White gas (known as *bencina blanca* or *nafta blanca*) and kerosene can be purchased from hardware stores in Mendoza (bring your own containers), and with a bit of asking and hunting, butane cartridges can also be located in sporting goods stores.

Strong duffel bags with locks will be needed to ensure that all of your food and equipment is delivered to base camp by the muleteers. The Horcones and Vacas Rivers are full of silt and will clog good water filters within a few strokes. It is possible to find clear water in the side streams that feed these rivers, but some type of strainer (such as coffee filters) should be carried in addition to a water purifying system.

Despite all of this talk about cold temperatures, the approach to base camp can be through debilitating heat and strong winds. So the approach uniform consists of a sun hat (perhaps with a "foreign legion" sun shield), sun glasses, T-shirt, shorts, wind breaker, wind pants, and hiking boots. A surprising number of climbers hike to base camp wearing their high-altitude mountaineering boots, however!

MAPS

Topographic maps of Aconcagua are published by the Argentine Instituto Geográfico Militar. Aconcagua is in the southeast corner of the 1:50,000 scale map "Cerro Aconcagua," catalog number 3369-7-4, but the "Las Cuevas" (3369-13-2), "Puente del Inca" (3369-14-1), and "Cerro Ameghino" (3369-8-3) maps are also needed to put all sides of the mountain into perspective. Once these four maps have been cut and pasted together, it becomes apparent that the only lines that match among the four sheets are the grid coordinates, and the contour lines, glaciers, and streams are a confusing mess on the southern and eastern sides of Aconcagua. These

four maps are only available in Buenos Aires from the sales office of the Instituto Geográfico Militar at Cabildo 301 (located near the Ministro Carranza subway station). These maps are available for viewing and photocopying at the army base at Puente del Inca.

Fortunately, the Argentine private sector now publishes climber's maps of Aconcagua with vertical aerial photographs showing the routes and landmarks encountered during the climb. These are available in Mendoza from bookshops, sporting goods stores, and the ubiquitous kiosks selling magazines and newspapers.

The American Alpine Club once published a map of Aconcagua. This is no longer available from the AAC, but a blueprint of this map is available from the South American Explorers Club, 126 Indian Creek Rd, Ithaca, NY 14850 (telephone: 607-277-0488).

The best road maps of Argentina are obtained from the Automóvil Club Argentino (ACA), located in Mendoza at the corner of Rivadavia and San Martín. Members of the American Automobile Association can obtain these maps, a road atlas, camping information, a tourist guidebook, and other publications at a discount from the ACA, upon presentation of their AAA card. AAA members are also eligible for discounts at ACA restaurants, motels, and campgrounds. ACA services are not really applicable to Aconcagua, but they can be handy for those who plan on touring Argentina (by either automobile or public transportation) before or after the climb.

FOOD

There are several large supermarkets in Mendoza offering similar products as supermarkets in North America. Climbing-type food available includes dry soups, dry potatoes, pudding mixes, dried milk, instant hot cereal, instant rice, dried fruits, dry salami, pasta, and processed cheese. While Argentina is famous for its beef, most Argentines seem to prefer it fresh, and the selection of canned meat seems to be limited to "canned meat product," sardines, and tuna. Bread is best obtained from a bakery. Most expeditions hire mules to carry their gear to base camp, and fresh produce and steaks have been served during the approach and at base camp.

Freeze-dried food is available in the sporting goods stores in Mendoza, but it is very expensive, more than three times what it would

cost in North America. Those who travel to Mendoza from Santiago should be forewarned that Chile has firm restrictions on importing not only fresh fruit, but also dried fruit, such as raisins. (A lot of North American winter fruit is imported from Chile.) It seems that Chilean customs has learned to search North American *andinistas* and confiscate their supply of gorp! This is best purchased in Mendoza.

CONSERVATION

Aconcagua receives a tremendous amount of human impact. Over two thousand climbers attempt the mountain each year, with almost seventy-five percent of them on the Normal Route. The Aconcagua Provincial Park has a campaign via the permit system to clean the mountain and keep it clean. Each group is issued numbered trash bags; the bags are checked at the end of the trip to assure that each group brings out its own trash. Packing out one's own rubbish is now not only common sense, but also a strictly enforced law on Aconcagua.

The best way for climbers to limit their impact is to reduce what they carry onto the mountain. A party that brings surplus gear, food, and fuel to cover every imaginable contingency will have a much more difficult time removing the leftovers from the mountain. Many well-intentioned (but naive) parties generously leave behind their surplus food and fuel at caches for other expeditions that may be in need of critical supplies. These caches are seldom used as intended, and instead end up as dumps high on the mountain. It is better to give surplus food and fuel *in person* to another party, who will then either use it or pack it out. But the best option of all is not to carry it onto the mountain in the first place.

A party should carry a *maximum* of 18 days of food and fuel on the Normal Route and no more than 20 days of supplies on the Polish Glacier. With the typical schedules outlined above, 15 days of supplies on the Normal Route and 18 days on the Polish Glacier should be ample. As a rough guideline, figure a maximum of 0.9 kilograms (2 pounds) of food per person per day and 0.125 liter (or quart) of white gas or kerosene per person per day.[11] For example, a party of four bound for the Normal Route with 90 kilograms (or 200 pounds) of food and 13 liters (or quarts) of fuel is carrying too much! For this party, 65 kilograms (143 pounds) of food and 9 liters (or quarts) of fuel should be plenty.

Another way to minimize impact is to repackage all food into plastic

bags. Bulky store packaging can add twenty-five percent to the net weight of food; for a climber, this packaging is dead weight which not only must be carried up the mountain but must also be carried down and out. It is much more efficient weight-wise to repackage all foodstuffs into plastic bags. When the food has been consumed, it is easy to collapse the bags into compact bundles and carry them down the mountain. Paper and cardboard can be burned, but it is messy, and the resulting piles of ash mark the route with sooty patches, in a similar manner that classic rock climbs are marked by patches of chalk. It is far more efficient, and more environmentally sound, to use plastic bags and carry them out instead of burning paper.

An ascent of Aconcagua involves a considerable investment of time and money. The goal of every climber is to reach the summit and return home safely. There is far less effort involved in removing one's own rubbish from the mountain than there is in reaching the summit. There is no reason why climbers cannot also make the commitment to leave the mountain clean. With proper planning and organization, it is not only possible but also easy to minimize each climber's impact on the mountain. All of us, i.e., *you and I,* must make the commitment to leave Aconcagua clean.

SEASONS AND WEATHER

Aconcagua is located at 32° 39' 13" South. This latitude is the same distance south of the equator that San Diego or Dallas is north of the equator. In the Southern Hemisphere, the seasons are reversed, and the best time of year to climb the mountain is during the austral summer, from December until early March. It follows that one can expect more snow and higher rivers early in the season, followed by increasingly drier conditions as the season progresses.

While Aconcagua is entirely within the Republic of Argentina, the Pacific Ocean is only 150 kilometers (90 miles) to the west. The mountain receives almost all of its bad weather during the austral summer from the moist, humid winds that blow from the west off of the Pacific Ocean. A typical scenario is that these winds are driven upward by the western slope of the Andes, where the air cools, condenses, and forms the lenticular cloud that covers the summit: the famous *viento blanco,* or white wind, a sign of snow and high winds at altitude. These westerly

winds can also generate fierce electrical storms during the summer. Don't underestimate this phenomenon; it is essential to descend to a lower altitude at the first sign of the *viento blanco.*

I have had bad luck predicting the weather on Aconcagua. The only general advice that I can give is that clouds and winds blowing from the north and west seem to precede bad weather, while winds and clouds moving out of the south and east seem to bring good weather. The park rangers and base camp managers at Plaza de Mulas rely on weather forecasts from broadcast radio stations in Chile. They add this data to their considerable experience on Aconcagua, and can give fairly accurate forecasts to climbers.

The peak climbing month (no pun intended) seems to be February, when the climbing conditions are reported to be the best. However, an increasing number of climbers seems to be on the mountain during Christmas; the rivers are much higher during this period, but there is also more snow on Aconcagua, making the climb more esthetic.

Some parties plan their climbs so their members can join two South American celebrations after climbing Aconcagua. Attending Carnival in Viña del Mar, Rio de Janeiro, Punta del Este, or Mar del Plata is an obvious way to celebrate an adventure on South America's highest peak. And the city of Mendoza also hosts the Argentine national wine festival over the first weekend in March. Those who plan to attend this event should make their hotel reservations six months to a year in advance.

HIGH-ALTITUDE HEALTH

The main health concerns on Aconcagua are the effects of high altitude. Different people have different reactions when exposed to altitude, and I continue to have different responses each time I climb above 4600 m (15,110 ft). This is undoubtedly due to several intervening variables for both myself and other people. On more than one occasion, I have seen Himalayan veterans flat on their backs, while less experienced climbers in the same party continued to set a new personal altitude record with each bounding stride taken upward. The major illnesses to watch out for include the following:

Acute mountain sickness occurs after too rapid an ascent to

1500–1800 m (5,000–6,000 ft). Headache, dizziness, drowsiness, shortness of breath, nausea, and sometimes vomiting are the classic symptoms of *la puna* or *la apunamiento,* Argentine slang for mountain sickness. The best cure is rest and descent to a lower elevation. At a lower altitude, the illness usually subsides fairly quickly, and the climb can be resumed after a day or two of rest.

High-altitude pulmonary edema is a serious, life-threatening medical emergency. It comes on rapidly, and has been known to cause death less than 40 hours after a rapid climb to 3000 m (10,000 ft). One subjective warning sign is to observe who is the most fit at the start of the climb. If that person's fitness decreases as he or she climbs higher, then he or she may contract it. Another warning sign is extreme weakness going uphill. High-altitude pulmonary edema is affected by cold, so keep yourself as warm as possible. The symptoms include a cough with bloody or foamy sputum, shortness of breath, general weakness, and a gurgling sound in the chest. If any of these symptoms appear, assume the worst and get the victim to a lower elevation as soon as possible. An authority on this illness, Dr. Charles S. Houston, has noted: "High altitude pulmonary edema may proceed rapidly to coma and death, or may improve with equal speed if the victim goes down only a few thousand feet after symptoms begin."[12] If the victim can't move under his or her own power, then *carry* him or her to a lower elevation. If oxygen is available, administer it. Some expeditions may have a portable hyperbaric chamber (such as the Gamow Bag). This increases the barometric pressure around the victim, simulating a lower altitude. Use of this is no substitute for descent, but it may be useful for treatment when descent is impossible due to weather or terrain.

Cerebral edema is not common (I have seen only one case of it) but is the most serious of the three. Symptoms include a severe headache, staggering, and hallucinations, and the condition can lead to coma and death. It rarely occurs below 4200 m (13,780 ft). As with pulmonary edema, *carry the victim* if necessary to a lower elevation to save his or her life!

The best medicine is prevention, and there are some things that climbers can do to minimize their risks of illness and improve their performance:

Slow ascent. The mountaineer's dictum, "Climb high, sleep low,"

is the best method to prevent altitude sickness. The crucial factor here is the *sleeping* altitude. Dr. Peter Hackett recommends, "Once above 3,000 meters, limit your net gain in altitude (your sleep altitude) to 300 meters per day (1,000 feet)."[13] On Aconcagua this is readily accomplished by relaying loads between camps. For example, carry a load of food and fuel to the higher campsite, deposit it there, and return to the lower camp to sleep; carry the rest of your equipment to the higher campsite the next day, and sleep there.

Drink, drink, drink some more! Water, that is. While dehydration does not cause mountain sickness, it decreases physical performance and the ability to generate heat from muscles, contributing to chilling and fatigue which may lead to altitude illness, as well as hypothermia and frostbite. Four liters or quarts per day is the minimum, and 6 liters or quarts per day is not too much. Think of water as a harmless recreational drug. I believe that it transforms my personality, making me more relaxed, more alert, and more attractive to members of the opposite sex.

Don't push yourself. Racing up Aconcagua is a very good way to bring on mountain sickness. Those who are young and fit are more susceptible to altitude illness simply because they climb faster, and therefore are more prone to fatigue and chilling. A slow, steady pace, such as the rest step, will carry you higher much better and easier than the "dash and crash" that seems to be the norm.

Don't drink alcohol. Even small amounts of alcohol seem to be detrimental to good acclimatization, in my experience. There is also some anecdotal evidence that alcohol may be a contributing factor to high-altitude cerebral edema. Besides, an overdose almost always results in some weird side effects!

Drugs. Many climbers take medication on the advice of their physicians to prevent or relieve the major symptoms of acute mountain sickness.[14] My two drugs of choice are water and descent. If I have a headache at altitude, I drink a liter (quart) of water. The headache is usually gone by the time I finish the liter. If I still have a headache an hour later, then I drink another liter, while descending.

Another major health concern is cold injury: **hypothermia and frostbite.** These are prevented not just by wearing warm clothing but

Drinking lots of water is one of the best ways to prevent mountain sickness.

also by proper body maintenance. Being well fed, well hydrated and well acclimatized are much more important than wearing and using state-of-the-art clothing and equipment. Those who do not take care of themselves will have trouble keeping warm in cold and windy weather. The hypothermia victim will become weak, cranky, and start to shiver uncontrollably. When the shivering stops, death is imminent. The victim should be placed in a tent, or at least out of the wind, and fed hot drinks and high-energy foods. If the victim is or has been shivering uncontrollably, it may be necessary to provide external heat with bottles filled with hot water and/or have someone strip off his or her clothes and climb into the sleeping bag with the victim.

While untreated hypothermia may be fatal in a short period of time, frostbite in this day and age is seldom fatal. However, it can leave one crippled for life. A few of my friends have suffered from deep frostbite while climbing some of the high mountains of the world, and after seeing their suffering (not to mention their medical bills), I can tell you that climbing to the summit of Aconcagua is not worth the loss of a single digit. As a general rule, if one's hands or feet haven't warmed up after one hour of climbing, then expect frostbite. The symptoms start with cold feet and/or hands and progress to pain. The pain is a warning sign to rewarm the extremity immediately. (Those who ignore the pain may suddenly feel "warm" hands and feet; in reality, their extremities have gone numb, and they have deep frostbite.) Rewarming is most easily done by placing the hands in someone's armpits, or placing the bare feet on someone's stomach, until the hands or feet feel warm. Don't hesitate to ask your partners for this service, and don't hesitate to offer it to the victim.

But it is too late to use this method to rewarm deep frostbite, marked by pale white skin that is ice hard. In this case, the best treatment is to *keep the hand or foot frozen* until rapid rewarming of the frozen extremity can be done in a warm (38 to 42 degrees C or 100 to 108 degrees F) bath, in a place where the victim's entire body can be kept warm during and after treatment and where the victim can be easily evacuated without walking on his or her feet. This is a painful treatment, and after rewarming, the victim *must be carried* to prevent further damage to the feet. Frostbite must be avoided at all costs, including the summit.

The Aconcagua Provincial Park rangers are responsible for rescues. At present, this service is only available on the Normal Route, with evacuation of the injured climber to Plaza de Mulas. The rangers maintain a supply of oxygen at Plaza de Mulas, along with other first aid supplies. Further evacuation to Puente del Inca is usually done by horse or mule, but in extraordinary circumstances the rangers are able to call for high-altitude helicopters. Evacuation beyond Plaza de Mulas, either by mule or helicopter, is the victim's financial responsibility.

GROUND TRANSPORTATION

Highway 7 leads south out of the city of Mendoza before turning west, climbing into the Andes, and eventually leading to Santiago. It is a major, paved highway with lots of traffic. There are many transportation options available between Mendoza and Puente del Inca.

Bus at Puente del Inca

Perhaps the easiest option is to hire a taxi, van, or small bus. This is the most expensive choice, and it is only cost effective with a large group (eight to twelve persons). But there are also some considerable advantages to this: it is easier to keep track of gear and equipment; the only schedule to meet is your own; stops can be easily arranged between Uspallata, Punta de Vacas, Los Penitentes, and Puente del Inca; and it is faster (Puente del Inca is 2 to 3 hours from Mendoza nonstop).

Most climbers take the twice-daily Expresso Uspallata bus that runs between the Mendoza bus station and Las Cuevas, the last Argentine town before the Chilean border. This bus leaves Mendoza at 6:00 A.M. and 10:00 A.M., and takes about 4 hours to arrive at Puente del Inca. Be sure to purchase the tickets at least one day ahead of time.

MULES

Mules are used to haul the expedition's impedimenta from the trailhead to the base camp. Aconcagua has been climbed many times without the use of mules, so this expensive service is not really essential for a successful climb; however, it may be helpful in dealing with heavy loads, long distances, and sometimes-difficult river crossings. A two-person party approaching the mountain via the Horcones Valley (i.e., the Normal Route) would typically need one pack mule (maximum load 60 kilograms or 132 pounds) and one muleteer on horseback. The mule will take 1 day to carry the food and equipment to Plaza de Mulas, while the climbers will typically take 2 days for this approach. An approach up the Vacas Valley (i.e., the Polish Glacier) would require one extra muleteer on horseback (due to the severe river crossings); the muleteers meet the climbers at each river crossing to ensure a safe passage. It follows that the Vacas Valley approach is more expensive than the Horcones Valley approach.

There are several options for locating muleteers. The simplest is to work through the outfitter who has made arrangements for the animals. Those who haven't hired an outfitter may instead contact one of the established, licensed packers who routinely serves Aconcagua expeditions; a current, up-to-date list is available from the Aconcagua Provincial Park office in Mendoza, where climbing permits are obtained. These

outfitters are based between Punta de Vacas and Puente del Inca, and their expensive rates are usually fixed (i.e., they are not open to bargaining). A packer can be contacted four to six weeks before the trip, telling him the approach route, entry and exit dates, and the number of animals needed, but this is not absolutely necessary. Be sure to note whether the price quoted is one way (*ida*) or round trip (*ida y vuelta*). A one-way price is not a problem for deliveries made to Plaza de Mulas because it is very easy (and much less expensive) to hire an unladen muleteer at that location to carry expedition equipment and refuse out to Puente del Inca. Also, the park ranger stationed at Plaza Argentina can make a radio call to the La Leña ranger to find out if any mules are headed up the Vacas and Relinchos Valleys, or even call for a muleteer to make a special trip.

Mules in the Horcones Valley

I like to think of the established packers as "FBOs," or fixed-base operators. Another, perhaps less expensive, option is the "FBNs," or fly-by-nights. These are the independent, unlicensed muleteers (who may be smugglers between assignments). They can be found near Puente del Inca or Punta de Vacas. One must have an excellent command of Argentine Spanish to strike a deal with these individuals and to ensure that both parties agree that the fee includes river crossings on mule or horseback for the climbers, as well as where and when the equipment will be delivered. It is best if all of this is written down by the packer, so the client can interpret the facts, times, dates, and places at leisure. Pay half of the agreed fee in advance, and pay the rest on delivery. It is best to have one's gear in durable duffel bags that can be locked, and ideally, one should travel with the mules for peace of mind regarding the safe delivery of the goods. In reality, the pack animals are much faster than the hikers, and the muleteers will wisely urge you to start hiking before the mules are loaded, to facilitate timely meetings at the river crossings and campsites.

HOW TO USE THIS BOOK

The following chapters describe the three major approaches, and then outline the climbing routes on Aconcagua from left to right from the perspective of each base camp site. The words "left" and "right" in the climbing route descriptions themselves are given from the perspective of facing the summit that each route ends atop. If this may be confusing, a cardinal direction is also offered, such as "left (southeast)." Elevations and measurements of latitude and longitude are provided throughout the route descriptions to assist climbers using both maps and GPS devices.

The difficulty of the individual pitches of technical routes has been graded using both the *Union Internationale des Associations d'Alpinisme* (UIAA) System and the Yosemite Decimal System (YDS). The UIAA System has been in existence since the 1960s, but it wasn't until 1989 that the UIAA actually created a table that compared the UIAA System with the YDS, as well as with the French, British, Australian, and German systems. This book uses the standards proclaimed by the UIAA in 1989, but the reader should be warned that there is no guarantee that these UIAA and YDS grades will actually match in the real world.

What follows is a list of all of the routes on Aconcagua, starting with what I believe to be the easiest route, and ending with the most difficult. This ranking is based only on my estimate of difficulty, and not exposure to objective dangers (such as avalanches and rockfall).

The Normal Route
Los Guías de Mendoza
Falso de los Polacos
Polish Glacier Route
Polish Glacier Direct Route
Directa
North Face Route
West Face Route
Aragonesa Variation of the Polish Glacier Direct Route
Ibáñez–Marmillod Route
Zabaleta Variation of the Ibáñez–Marmillod Route
Mendocino Variation of the Ibáñez–Marmillod Route
East Glacier Route
Southeast Ridge Route
Central Route
Esteban Escaiola Route
Argentine Route
La Tapia del Felipe
La Ruleta Rusa
Slovene Variation of the French Route
French Route
Messner Variation of the French Route
Lower Argentine Variation of the French Route
Japanese Variation of the French Route
Upper Argentine Variation of the French Route
Sun Line Route
French Direct Route
Slovene 1986 Route
Slovene Route
Polish Variation of the Slovene Route

Chapter Three

HORCONES VALLEY APPROACH

The Horcones Valley is used to approach the Normal Route, as well as the routes on the west and southwest sides of Aconcagua. And the lower part of the Horcones Valley is followed as the initial approach to the routes on the South Face. This approach starts from Puente del Inca (2720 m, 8,924 ft; 32° 49' 24"S, 69° 54' 36"W), a small town located about 182 kilometers (113 miles) from Mendoza via Highway 7, and is served by local buses from Mendoza. The name Puente del Inca comes from the natural bridge that crosses the Río de las Cuevas. This bridge is quite impressive, and automobiles and small trucks routinely drove across it until recently. There is a hotel at Puente del Inca, and also some hostels with dormitory-style accommodations as well as restaurants. There are also hotels, hostels, and restaurants at Los Penitentes (2580 m, 8,460 ft; 32° 50' 23"S, 69° 50' 06"W), a ski area that is 6 kilometers (3.7 miles) east of Puente del Inca. There is a destroyed resort across the bridge (the victim of an avalanche) along with a church that miraculously survived the avalanche. The ruins of the resort serve as a climber's campground (with hot springs!). It is wise to keep someone in the camp to prevent theft.

The muleteers are usually very busy during the height of the climbing season, and there may be a 1- or 2-day delay prior to starting the approach. This time can help with acclimatization, and many parties do some local hikes in order to obtain views of Aconcagua or Tupungato, the next major mountain to the south of Puente del Inca. One diversion (if the road is open) is to negotiate one's way onto a tourist bus to see *Cristo Redentor*, or Christ of the Andes, a statue made from Argentine armaments that is on the Argentine–Chilean border at an altitude of 3832 m (12,572 ft). The main attraction of this trip is not necessarily the statue; while the statue is huge, it is dwarfed by the magnificent natural surroundings. Less than a kilometer to the east of Puente del Inca is the cemetery for *andinistas* (you don't have to major in English to understand

Cemetery for andinistas

symbolism). It should be stressed that not everyone buried in this cemetery died on Aconcagua. One of the more prominent graves is that of Nicolás Plantamura, who made the first Argentine ascent of Aconcagua in 1934.

There is a small army base at Puente del Inca, with ever-vigilant guards. Photography of the base or anything else military-related is prohibited, and this regulation is strictly enforced.

The actual trailhead for the Horcones Valley is at the Horcones Ranger Station, northwest of Puente del Inca. This is reached by driving west from Puente del Inca along Highway 7, bypassing the customs house, for approximately 4 kilometers (2.4 miles) to where a dirt road leads north another 2 kilometers (1.2 miles) to the start of the trail. Most outfitters drive their clients (and even other outfitters' clients) to the roadhead. Those hiking walk 1 kilometer (0.6 mile) to the customs station where several trails lead northwest for 3.5 kilometers (2.1 miles) to the roadhead and the ranger station (2850 m, 9,350 ft; 32° 48' 36"S,

69° 56' 30"W). The park rangers stationed here will check permits and issue litter bags. The trail (in reality, a road in this area) starts out on the left (west) bank of the Horcones River, passes tiny Laguna Horcones, and soon crosses to the right bank on a suspension bridge and stays on the east side of the river for 6.2 kilometers (3.7 miles) to the Confluencia Crossing (3320 m, 10,892 ft; 32° 45' 36"S, 69° 58' 18"W). The crossing of the Lower Horcones has been made much easier with the installation of a footbridge. Go to the left and stay to the left beyond this footbridge and hike 0.8 kilometer (0.5 mile) to Confluencia Camp (3320 m, 10,892 ft; 32° 45' 12"S, 69° 58' 24"W), the traditional first night's campsite for the Horcones Valley approach. It is necessary to cross a stream to reach the campsite. A provincial park ranger is stationed here. Those camping at Confluencia Camp can hike upstream (instead of returning to the Confluencia Crossing) for 2.2 kilometers (1.3 miles) to rejoin the main trail at Confluencia Fork (3500 m, 11,482 ft; 32° 44' 24"S, 69° 59' 18"W).

Confluencia Camp can be bypassed by turning right immediately after Confluencia Crossing. The trail remains on the right (east) bank of

Bridge across the Horcones River

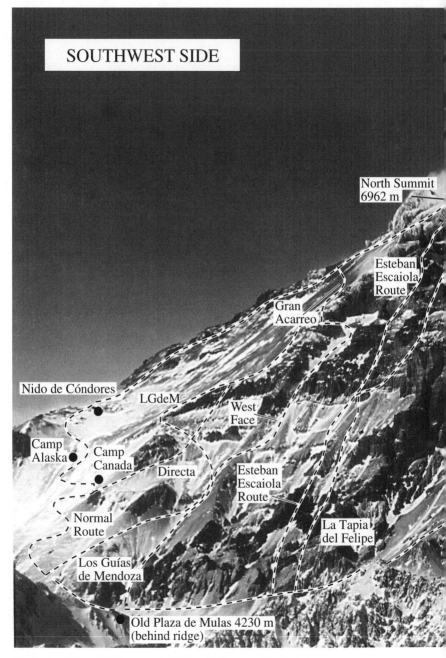

SOUTHWEST SIDE

North Summit
6962 m

Esteban
Escaiola
Route

Gran
Acarreo

Nido de Cóndores

LGdeM

West
Face

Camp
Alaska

Camp
Canada

Directa

Esteban
Escaiola
Route

Normal
Route

La Tapia
del Felipe

Los Guías
de Mendoza

Old Plaza de Mulas 4230 m
(behind ridge)

Photo by Albert W. Stevens, © *National Geographic Society*

Piedra Grande at Colorado

the main Horcones River, passes a wet meadow, and then arrives at the fork leading back to Confluencia Camp after 2.7 kilometers (1.7 miles). The trail soon enters the Colorado area (marked by the red dust on hiking boots) and the last major landmark, Piedra Grande (Big Rock) (32° 44' 19"S, 70° 00' 00"W), 1.1 kilometers (0.7 mile) beyond the Confluencia Fork. What follows is a long, flat stretch of trail, devoid of landmarks. After 3.3 kilometers (2 miles) beyond Piedra Grande, the jagged Quebrada Sargento Mas enters from the right (32° 41' 30"S, 70° 01' 30"W). Just beyond this point is Playa Ancha, where the main Horcones River continually changes its course (depending on the time of day, season, or year). It may be necessary to make as many as five fords across the braided channels over the next 3.9 kilometers (2.3 miles). The Ibáñez campsite (3960 m, 12,992 ft; 32° 41' 30"S, 70° 03' 06"W) is encountered on the right (east) bank after these fords, and the trail continues another 3.7 kilometers (2.2 miles) to Lower Plaza de Mulas (4050 m, 13,287 ft; 32° 39' 30"S, 70° 03' 18"W), marked by a destroyed building. Continue another 0.5 kilometer (0.3 mile) to a fork (32° 39' 18"S, 70° 03' 30"W) that leads left and up a very steep trail to Hotel Refugio. The

main trail goes to the right and makes the Subida Brava, or in English, the Hardy Climb. The trail makes a steep, continuous 0.7-kilometer (0.4-mile) climb to Old Plaza de Mulas (4230 m, 13,877 ft; 32° 39' 00"S, 70° 03' 12"W). New Plaza de Mulas is 0.4 kilometer (0.2 mile) beyond. This last section will exhaust anyone who has hiked the 23 kilometers (14 miles) and 1420 meters (4,700 feet) of gain in one day from the trailhead.

New Plaza de Mulas (4270 m, 14,009 ft; 32° 38' 54"S, 70° 03' 24"W) is the new base camp for the Normal Route. Old Plaza de Mulas received a tremendous amount of use and abuse, but the park rangers and outfitters have wisely moved the camp to a new location. Potable water is available during warm afternoons from small streams immediately north of the camp, and outhouses are in place. Another base camp site is at Hotel Refugio, about 1 kilometer (0.6 mile) west of New Plaza de Mulas (4370 m, 14,337 ft; 32° 39' 06"S, 70° 03' 48"W). This is a real hotel with hot and cold running water, showers, sanitary facilities, bunk rooms, a cooking area, and a dining room serving real food. It is possible to camp near the hotel and use the facilities, as needed, for a fee. The hotel also has porters that will carry 25-kilogram (55-pound) loads of food and equipment as high as Berlin Camp.

New Plaza de Mulas

Hotel Refugio

Those who are seeking a bit more of a wilderness experience may want to explore the Horcones Glacier to the north of Plaza de Mulas. A prominent peak in this area is Cerro Cuerno (5462 m; 17,920 ft), a moderately difficult ice climb.

THE NORMAL ROUTE

This route was first explored by Paul Güssfeldt in 1883, and the first ascent was made by Matthias Zurbriggen during Edward FitzGerald's expeditions to Aconcagua and Tupungato in 1897. It is also known as "The Northwest Route" because part of it follows the Northwest Ridge of the mountain. It is by far the most popular route, and among my friends I refer to it as "The Freeway Route." It presents minimal technical difficulties. Dogs have been taken to the summit, and motorcycles have been ridden as high as 6600 m (21,653 ft) via this route (ugh!). While there are no permanent snowfields, each climber should be equipped with good, cold-weather, double mountaineering boots, crampons, and an ice axe. There are some huts, but most of these are in disrepair, so stormproof, four-season tents should be carried.

Cerro Cuerno from the Normal Route

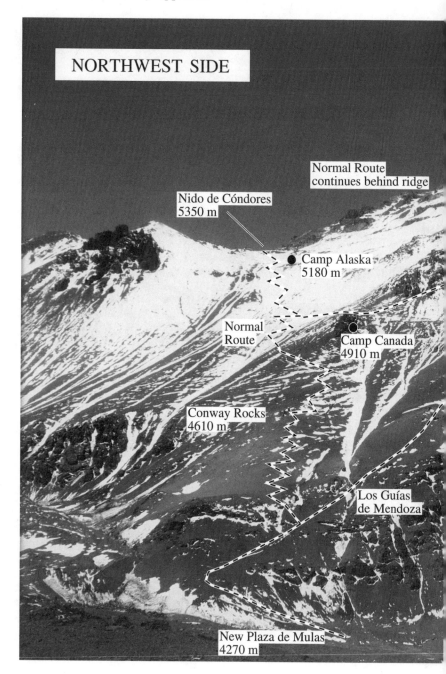

NORTHWEST SIDE

Normal Route continues behind ridge

Nido de Cóndores 5350 m

Camp Alaska 5180 m

Normal Route

Camp Canada 4910 m

Conway Rocks 4610 m

Los Guías de Mendoza

New Plaza de Mulas 4270 m

North Summit
6962 m

Canaleta

Gran
Acarreo

LGdeM

Directa

West
Face
Route

Old Plaza de Mulas
4230 m

Follow the well-worn trail that leads to the north from Plaza de Mulas. The trail climbs up the steep slope that is east of the Horcones Glacier before turning right and climbing a steep scree slope with long, shallow switchbacks. Near the top of this slope some flat spots offer exposed campsites among the Conway Rocks (4610 m, 15,124 ft; 32° 38' 48"S; 70° 03' 00"W). Another site is known as Camp Canada (4910 m, 16,108 ft; 32° 38' 42"S, 70° 02' 36"W). This is a flat spot atop a promontory marked by some rock pinnacles, about a half-kilometer (0.3 mile) to the south of the main trail. The next campsite is a large, exposed, sloping platform: Camp Alaska (5180 m, 16,995 ft; 32° 38' 24"S, 70° 02' 12"W), also known as Cambio de Pendiente (Change of Slope). From Camp Alaska, the trail climbs a short distance to the south before turning left (east) to avoid a field of *penitentes*. There is a hut up and off to the far right (south) of the trail: the Refugio Antartida Argentina is at 5400 m (17,716 ft), but this tiny shelter is in ruins. Most expeditions bypass these campsites and head directly for Nido de Cóndores (5350 m, 17,552 ft; 32° 38' 06"S, 70° 01' 48"W), a large, flat area with some rocks serving as wind breaks. There is a small pond here, and water can be obtained from it on warm afternoons. Most climbers take 6 to 8 hours to hike to Nido de Cóndores from Plaza de Mulas.

Conway Rocks along the Normal Route

Camp Canada

Climbing the Normal Route

Looking southeast from Nido de Cóndores one can see the upper part of Aconcagua across a vast scree field known as the Gran Acarreo, which can be loosely translated as the Long Haul. While this is the route that Zurbriggen followed in 1898, it cannot be recommended as either an ascent or descent route. Aside from the exhaustive nature of climbing scree, this exposed field offers no shelter in the event of bad weather, and, as Paddy Sherman wisely observed, "It was up there that Zurbriggen went, and it must have been a dumb, stupid, mindless day to weaken him so much that he would follow that route to the top."[15]

The better route at first goes east from Nido de Cóndores, then turns to the south and ascends the subtle crest of the ridge to the three huts that mark the Berlin Camp (5780 m, 18,963 ft; 32° 38' 18"S, 70° 01' 18"W). This camp is marked as "Plantamura" on some maps because the first hut constructed here in 1946 was named after Nicolás Plantamura. The second, slightly larger hut is now known as Libertad (it was named "Eva Perón" after it was built in 1951), and the most recently constructed hut was constructed by some climbers from Berlin in memory of a friend who had died on Aconcagua. These tiny huts are in various stages of disrepair, and they are usually used as cooking areas for climbers camped at Berlin. Most

Berlin Camp

Nido de Cóndores

parties take 2 to 3 hours to climb to Berlin Camp from Nido de Cóndores. Berlin Camp is the usual high camp for most parties on the Normal Route.

From Berlin Camp the route at first heads left and continues up the vague ridge. It passes another campsite known as White Rocks at 6250 m (20,505 ft; 32° 38' 24"S, 70° 01' 18"W). This site may be preferable to Berlin, as it receives less use and offers more shelter, with tent sites located among large boulders and small cliffs. The route continues up and then slightly to the right to reach the Independencia hut (*Refugio Independencia*) at 6400 m (20,997 ft; 32° 38' 42"S, 70° 00' 58"W), reportedly the highest alpine refuge in the world. It was built in 1951, formerly named after Juan Perón, but this hut is also in ruins, and many benighted climbers have bivouacked here following a late return from the summit. From the Independencia hut the route continues up and right, crossing the Cresta del Viento (Windy Crest), and heads across the upper part of the Gran Acarreo to the infamous Canaleta. The Canaleta is the most notorious part of the Normal Route. It is a 400-meter (1,300-foot) 33-degree chute filled with disagreeably loose rocks. At some places it consists of mind-numbing scree, while in others the chute features rocks too large to be classified as scree but too small to be called talus,

White Rocks campsite

but still loose just the same. This challenge is overcome not by any technical skill, but rather by superior mental and physical stamina necessary to keep moving despite losing 1 meter of progress for every 2 meters gained. The terrain seems to be more solid on the right side of the Canaleta. The Canaleta ends atop the Cresta del Guanaco, the ridge that connects the lower South Summit with the higher, North Summit of Aconcagua. Follow the ridge crest up to the small, sloping summit plateau, where an aluminum cross marks the top (6962 m, 22,841 ft; 32° 39' 13"S, 70° 00' 45"W). Most parties take from 7 to 10 hours to climb to the summit from the Berlin Camp.

Those who climb Aconcagua by another route may need some guidance to descend the Normal Route. It is not really necessary to follow the Cresta del Guanaco; one can descend straight into the Canaleta from the summit plateau. Slide down the Canaleta, gradually turning to the right, aiming for the relatively flat ground beneath the North Face of the mountain. (Don't continue straight down the Gran Acarreo to Nido de Cóndores; it is easy to get lost on this wide, featureless slope that

Ameghino and the Polish Glacier as seen from White Rocks

The Independencia hut

offers no shelter.) Head to the right (northeast) across the Cresta del Viento to the tiny Independencia shelter, which serves as a landmark. Move to the right (east) side of the ridge, and follow the good use trail down to Berlin Camp. One can traverse to the east (right) to the Polish Glacier between the Independencia hut and the Berlin Camp.

LOS GUÍAS DE MENDOZA

This could be considered as a variation to the Normal Route, but it is a completely independent line and doesn't meet the Freeway Route until the base of the Canaleta. It was first climbed on February 12, 1994, over a period of 12 days by Alejandro Randis, Rodolfo Gabrielli (then the Governor of the Province of Mendoza), Arturo Lafalla (the next Governor of Mendoza), Daniel Rodríguez, Jorge Giaquinta, Carlos Santilli, and Domingo Alvarez. Leave the Normal Route below Conway Rocks and climb up and right across the lower West Face of the mountain. Ascend the left side of the chute on the lower West Face, going above the level of a series of small cliffs, and then traverse up and left, passing immediately beneath a higher, larger cliff to a campsite at 5150 m (16,896 ft). (This campsite is above Camp Canada and southwest of Camp Alaska, and the Normal Route seems to be the best approach to this site, rather than the route of the first ascent party.) Continue climbing left and up from the camp, passing the left side of a large buttress that leads north from the West Face, to the Gran Acarreo. Climb the right side of the Gran Acarreo to another campsite at 5750 m (18,864 ft). The route continues up the right side of the Gran Acarreo, with a few detours around cliffs, to the base of the Canaleta, which is then followed to the summit.

DIRECTA

This route was first climbed in April 1991 by Luis López Soriano and Angel Martin Martínez. Leave the Normal Route at Camp Canada, pass the rocks above the camp on their right sides, and climb to the bottom of a couloir in the middle of the rock buttress that leads north from the West Face. The bottom of the couloir features UIAA III (YDS 5.4) rock, and its upper section has an angle up to 50 degrees. Continue up Los Guías de Mendoza to the base of the Canaleta.

Camp Canada from the Normal Route

WEST FACE ROUTE

This route was first climbed over a period of 6 days in January 1965 by an American party including Dick Hill, Ralph Mackey, and Gene Mason. It leads to the upper part of the Normal Route, and it is an interesting variation, but it is composed of loose, rotten rock. Head east from Old Plaza de Mulas and ascend a chute on the northern portion of the West Face. There is a campsite at 5200 m (17,000 ft) near the top of this lower chute. Move to the right over talus to a short (10 meters; 30 feet), vertical ice couloir at 5500 m (18,000 ft). Climb this couloir, and continue up the higher chute. This higher, snow-filled chute leads to a system of ledges and steep couloirs that lead up and left to a small notch at 5800 m (19,000 ft). This notch leads to the Gran Acarreo. Ascend the Gran Acarreo to meet the Normal Route at the base of the Canaleta, and follow the Normal Route to the summit.

ESTEBAN ESCAIOLA ROUTE

This route makes a direct ascent of the West Face of Aconcagua. It was climbed in 1991 by Daniel Varela and Antonio Mir. Go south from Plaza de Mulas and begin by climbing a prominent rock ridge on the lower part of the West Face. After five and a half pitches (nothing more difficult than UIAA III; YDS 5.4), one reaches the top of the cliff and a campsite at 4800 m (15,747 ft). Continue by climbing the scree slopes that mark the middle of the West Face to the base of the upper cliffs, aiming for a prominent snow and ice couloir. The couloir starts at an angle of 35 to 40 degrees and progressively becomes steeper. Near 5800 m (19,000 ft), a vertical section is encountered with UIAA IV + (YDS 5.6) rock. This is followed by several 25-meter (80-foot) vertical sections to 6300 m (20,669 ft) where the couloir becomes vertical for one and a half pitches. Continue climbing the 60-degree (YDS 5.7) upper slopes of the couloir, to where it ends high on the West Face. Move to the right and continue up the face to the South Summit. Follow the Cresta del Guanaco to the higher North Summit.

A minor variation was made by Brian Asbury and Glen Frank in December 1995. Instead of climbing the initial lower ridge, they hiked up the loose scree slopes to the left of the ridge to the foot of the couloir.

LA TAPIA DEL FELIPE

This route is also known as the Mendocino Route and the West Wall. It was first climbed in January 1988 by Argentines Daniel Alessio and Daniel Rodríguez, who placed three camps during the first ascent. Begin by climbing a steep chute at the base of the main West Face. From the top of this chute, move up and right, across the scree slope in the middle of the West Face, keeping to the right of the couloir that marks the Esteban Escaiola Route. Instead of climbing the couloir, continue up and right across a rock face to a 70-degree, 35-meter (115-foot) frozen waterfall, followed by another ice cascade at a 90-degree angle and 45 meters (150 feet) high. The rest of the route continues through snowfields with connecting steps and gullies of rotten rock (UIAA IV to VI; YDS 5.3 to 5.9). This route ends high along the Southwest Ridge.

IBÁÑEZ–MARMILLOD ROUTE

This route is also known as the Southwest Ridge and La Canaleta de Grajales. It traverses across the lower west and southwest faces of Aconcagua before climbing a huge couloir that leads onto the crest of the Southwest Ridge. It was first climbed on January 23, 1953, by Federico Marmillod, Dorly Marmillod, Francisco Ibáñez, and Fernando Grajales over a period of 7 days.

At first, head south from Plaza de Mulas before climbing up and to the right across the scree slopes that mark the lower and middle West Face. These slopes eventually lead to some small rock cliffs on the lower southwest slope of the mountain. This is the site of Camp 1 (5300 m; 17,390 ft). Continue traversing for 2 to 3 kilometers (1.2 to 1.8 miles) to the southeast, along the bottom edge of a cliff that surrounds this side of the mountain like a belt, toward the Southwest Ridge. Looking up, one can see the huge Grajales Couloir descending from above this cliff. Continue past this landmark almost to the crest of the lower Southwest Ridge, to a deep and narrow chute, partly filled with snow and ice, approximately 100 meters (328 feet) high. Ascend this chute to the base of the lower towers along the crest of the Southwest Ridge, very close to Cerro Piramidal (Point 6009 m; 19,714 ft). Turn left (north) at the base of these towers and descend about 200 meters (656 feet) down a rocky

WEST SIDE

North Summit
6962 m

Canaleta

Normal
Route

Gran Acarreo

West
Face
Route

South Summit
6930 m

La Tapia
del Felipe

Esteban
Escaiola
Route

slope to a ledge that leads to the Grajales Couloir. Camp 2 is located here under an overhanging rock, at 5700 m (18,700 ft).

Climb the Grajales Couloir, at first by means of a smooth rock slope and then over hard snow, and finally a narrow 45-degree ice couloir between two rock walls. The Grajales Couloir gradually widens and ends at a cliff at the head of an open slope. Bypass the cliff by traversing up and to the left; the site of Camp 3 (6400 m; 21,000 ft) is in this area. Continue climbing the slope and small ridges above to meet the crest of the Southwest Ridge at Point 6707 m (22,004 ft).

Follow the crest of the Southwest Ridge, which is wide with patches of snow among loose rock, to the South Summit of Aconcagua (6930 m; 22,736 ft). Descend the Cresta del Guanaco, passing the guanaco skeleton along the way, until meeting the upper part of the Canaleta on the Normal Route. Ascend the Canaleta to the higher, true summit of Aconcagua.

ZABALETA VARIATION OF THE IBÁÑEZ–MARMILLOD ROUTE

This variation to the Southwest Ridge was climbed over a period of 5 days by Martín Zabaleta, Xabier Erro, and Joan Hugas on January 2, 1979. Traverse southeast from Camp 1 toward the crest of the lower Southwest Ridge for about 1 kilometer (0.6 mile). Climb the cliff above by means of a short, moderately difficult couloir. This ends at the base of a smaller, secondary cliff. Traverse left along the base of this cliff to a ledge that leads up to a short snow chute. Follow the chute to the Grajales Couloir, and continue up the Southwest Ridge route.

MENDOCINO VARIATION OF THE IBÁÑEZ–MARMILLOD ROUTE

This variation was first climbed in 1982 by Sergio Buslio and Carlos Sansoni. It begins low in the Horcones Valley by making a tiresome ascent of the Quebrada Sargento Mas to its head. Go left and climb onto the sloping bench between the first and second rock bands on the south face of Cerro Piramidal. Make a horizontal traverse across this steep bench toward Cerro Piramidal's southwest ridge. At one point this traverse is blocked by an 8-meter (26-foot) high wall; this is best overcome by a

direct, though exposed, assault (UIAA IV; YDS 5.5). This traverse eventually leads to the crest of the southwest ridge of Cerro Piramidal, where the ridge is followed to the summit of Cerro Piramidal. Follow the north ridge of Cerro Piramidal down; at one point a 20-meter (65-foot) rappel must be made along the ridge crest. This is followed by a gradual descending traverse to the west to meet the Ibáñez–Marmillod Route at 5700 m (18,700 ft).

In the Lower Horcones Valley

Chapter Four

SOUTH FACE APPROACH

The South Face of Aconcagua is approached via the Lower Horcones Valley. While the South Face has the most difficult routes on the mountain, the Lower Horcones Valley should not be completely ignored by trekkers. It is the shortest and most scenic of the three valleys used to approach Aconcagua. The first part of the approach passes through fields of rocks with fossils. As it climbs higher the route passes next to the Lower Horcones Glacier, with views of crevasses and seracs. It ends at the base of the South Face of Aconcagua, one of the great mountain walls of the world.

The first part of the approach is the same as for the Normal Route: follow the trail from the Horcones Ranger Station for 6.2 kilometers (3.7 miles) to Confluencia, where the drainage of the Lower Horcones Glacier meets the main Horcones River. Instead of crossing the bridge at Confluencia, remain on the right (east) bank of the river and climb up into the Lower Horcones Valley. The path remains on the eastern side of the stream and glacier for 11 kilometers (6.6 miles) to Plaza Francia at 4100 m (13,451 ft; 32° 40' 37"S, 69° 58' 45"W), the traditional base camp site for the routes on the South Face. The Poincenot hut was once located near Plaza Francia, but the hut is now in ruins.

The following routes on the South Face are described from left to right (west to east) across the face.

SUN LINE ROUTE

This route was first climbed over a period of 2 days on January 12, 1988, by Slavko Sveticic and Milan Romih. It follows the crest (more or less) of the Southwest Ridge to the South Summit of Aconcagua. It doesn't meet the Ibáñez–Marmillod Route until near the South Summit. The first ascent party approached the ridge from the Lower Horcones Glacier, and its extreme technical nature (90-degree ice with rock pitches of UIAA VII (YDS 5.10+)) places the description of this route here, with the South Face routes.

Abbreviations: UAV: Upper Argentine Variation; JV: Japanese Variation; LAV: Lower Argentine Variation; FDR: French Direct Route; S1986V: Slovene 1986 Variation; UG: Upper Glacier; MG: Middle Glacier; LG: Lower Glacier

SOUTH FACE

JV

S1986V

Southeast Ridge

MG

Argentine
Route

FDR

Pasic Glacier

LAV

Slovene
Variation

La Ruleta Rusa

French
Route

LG

Central
Route

Photo by Albert W. Stevens, © National Geographic Society

Climb to the pass southeast of Cerro Piramidal, Portezuelo Sargento Mas, from the Lower Horcones Glacier. Traverse along the southwest side of the crest (UIAA IV; YDS 5.5) to a campsite at 5300 m (17,388 ft). Continue traversing up and left to a couloir that breaks the first line of cliffs on the right side of the south face of Cerro Piramidal. Climb the couloir (85 degrees), and then make a diagonal traverse up and right over 50- to 60-degree slopes to a chute that is near the crest of the Southeast Ridge. This 70-degree chute is followed by a UIAA V (YDS 5.7) rock pitch that is almost on the crest of the Southeast Ridge.

Overcoming the final headwall of the south face of Cerro Piramidal is next. Begin by making an almost horizontal traverse across 60- to 70-degree snow and ice slopes to the base of a right-ascending ramp system on the final headwall. This ramp system is the crux of the route with up to 90-degree ice and UIAA VII (YDS 5.10+) rock. The ramp ends atop a small snowfield on the crest of the Southeast Ridge. Follow the ridge upward (UIAA III; YDS 5.4) to the summit of Cerro Piramidal.

Follow the crest of the Southwest Ridge from the summit of Cerro Piramidal. Bypass the second tower by traversing up and left (UIAA V; YDS 5.7), followed by a 60-degree snow/ice chute behind the tower that leads back onto the crest of the ridge. The third tower is overcome by remaining on the ridge crest (UIAA V; 5.7). Continue following the ridge to the South Summit of Aconcagua.

Milan Romih was injured during the ascent of Cerro Piramidal, and it is interesting to note that Slavko Sveticic soloed the upper part of this route, and then descended the French Route on the South Face.

SLOVENE ROUTE

This extreme route climbs the south buttress to the South Summit. It was first climbed in 1982 over a period of 9 days of bad weather by Zlatko Gantar, twin brothers Pavel and Peter Podgornik, and Ivan Rejc. Most of this route consists of climbing on extremely loose, but frozen, rock, and the first ascent party was forced to climb for the most part at night to take advantage of the freezing temperatures.

The route begins at the far, left-hand side of the face, to the left of the major central couloir. The first pitch is on loose rock (UIAA V; YDS

5.7) followed by a 50-meter (165-foot) vertical ice couloir. This leads to a 50-degree field of penitentes; go up and right over this field to a chute at 65 degrees. From the top of this chute, cross another penitente field (60 degrees) to a steep couloir. The first ascent party reported that this couloir consisted of black ice at 75 degrees and ended at another steep field of penitentes. Cross the penitentes by going up and right, followed by another steep ice couloir. The first ascent party found their first good campsite at the top of this couloir after 3 days of climbing.

Traverse up and left across some more penitentes, aiming for the left-hand side of the rock band that looms overhead. Bypass the rock band on its left side, and climb straight up the 65-degree slope toward the base of the seracs above. Traverse up and right over 45- to 55-degree slopes to the highest reach of this snowfield, where the first ascent party had a camp at the base of a rock cliff.

Traverse left along a ledge of rotten but verglassed rock (UIAA V +; YDS 5.8) and climb onto the next snowfield, at an angle of 50 degrees. Go up and right over this snowfield (there was a campsite in this area), over the crest of the buttress to a vertical couloir in a cliff of red rock. Climb this couloir, and the following wide snowfield, to the overhanging rock band that is the crux of the climb. This is 20 meters (66 feet) high, with a severe overhang, followed by 10 meters (33 feet) of vertical ice (UIAA VI, A3; YDS 5.9, A3); it took the first ascent party 2 days to overcome this obstacle. After the crux, go up and left over 50- to 55-degree slopes to the headwall beneath the South Summit. The headwall is UIAA IV (YDS 5.5), followed by easier climbing to the summit.

POLISH VARIATION OF THE SLOVENE ROUTE

This variation to the 1982 Slovene Route was climbed in late January 1987 by Leszek Cichy and Ryszard Kolakowski. They found the lower part of the original route to be covered with flowing cascades of water. The variation climbs the face to the right of the lower portion of the Yugoslav Route, meeting it at the Yugoslav's "first good campsite." Difficulties of UIAA V + (YDS 5.8) and ice to 90 degrees were reported in addition to severe loose rock; both climbers suffered from rockfall injuries during this climb. This variation of the Slovene Route may be the most difficult route on Aconcagua.

SOUTH FACE

South Summit
6930 m

Upper
Glacier

Slovene
Route

Lower
Argentine
Variation

Slovene
Route

Slovene
Variation

Polish
Variation

Messner
Variation

North Summit
6962 m

Upper
Argentine

French Route

Central Route

Argentine Route

Pasic Glacier

Middle
Glacier

French
Dircet Route

area of detail sketch

French
Route

La Ruleta Rusa

Lower
Glacier

© 1994 Dee Molenaar

Abbreviations: SV: Slovene Variation; PV: Polish Variation; UAV: Upper Argentine Variation; JV: Japanese Variation; LAV: Lower Argentine Variation; FDR: French Direct Route; S1986V: Slovene 1986 Variation; UG: Upper Glacier; MG: Middle Glacier; LG: Lower Glacier

Photo by Albert W. Stevens, © National Geographic Society

FRENCH ROUTE

This was the first route established on the South Face, climbing the central buttress. It was first climbed on February 25, 1954, by Andrien Dagory, Guy Poulet, Edmond Denis, Robert Pagarot, Pierre Lasueur, and Lucien Berardini, with the final assault taking 7 days. Today most parties take 3 days.

This is one of the most coveted big wall routes in the world. In recent years, most parties have started by taking the Slovene Variation, continued up the French Route, and finished via the Messner Variation. This route description is of the 1954 French Route, and the variations climbed since then follow.

From Plaza Francia quickly (**avalanche danger**) head west along the base of the wall to the foot of the central buttress. Begin by climbing a broad chute that is to the right of the cliffs at the toe of the central buttress, but far to the left of the big couloir that marks the Lower Glacier on the South Face. At the head of the chute, go up and right along a ledge system to a point very exposed to avalanches falling from the Middle Glacier. Go straight up the left edge of this exposed section to a

Approaching the Lower Horcones Glacier

large band of grey and yellow rock. Follow this up and to the left away from the section exposed to avalanches. When the climbing becomes steep and more difficult, traverse to the right for 50 meters (165 feet) to a contact zone of yellow and black rocks. This is the landmark for a system of ledges that lead up and left to the crest of the central buttress. Follow the crest of the buttress upward to the site of the first camp (4500 m; 14,764 ft), approximately 4 hours from Plaza Francia.

The real technical challenges begin here. Continue up for 50 meters (165 feet) along the crest of the buttress, over loose rock to a short section of more solid, black rock; this 8-meter (26-ft) section varies from UIAA IV to VI (YDS 5.5 to 5.9), depending on snow cover. This is followed by 120 meters (400 feet) of UIAA III (YDS 5.4) rock to a series of couloirs (to 45 degrees), ramps, and ledges that lead for 250 to 300 meters (800 to 1,000 feet) to the base of the Great Towers. The first pitch (UIAA III–IV; YDS 5.4–5.5) leads to the base of a narrow, perhaps icy chimney, located to the right of a frozen waterfall. Climb the chimney for two pitches (to UIAA VI; YDS 5.9: there are many fixed pitons in the chimney); it may be necessary to haul packs near its top. The chimney ends atop the Great Towers. Go left and drop down about 5 meters (16 feet) into the couloir that feeds the frozen waterfall. Ascend the couloir for 150 meters (500 feet) to the bottom of the Middle Glacier. There are some campsites here at 5100 m (16,732 ft), approximately 8 hours from the campsite at 4500 m (14,764 ft).

Climb the 40- to 50-degree left side of the Middle Glacier to the 200-meter (656-foot) high rock cliff at its head; the base of this is at 5800 m (19,028 ft) and has been used as a campsite. This is an exposed, poorly protected cliff (more than one climber has stressed to me that three No. 2–3½ Friends are needed for protection in this section). It collects a lot of snow after a storm, and mixed climbing increases its difficulty. The cliff is overcome by first stemming a short, difficult (UIAA VI; YDS 5.9) chimney, with some ice-covered overhangs, followed by a huge rock slab with roofs. Two more pitches of easier climbing lead to the base of the Upper Glacier and the Ice Nose. This vertical ice wall may be from 15 to 50 meters (50 to 165 feet) high, depending on the snow/ice conditions, and many parties have had to resort to direct-aid climbing over ice. The top of this ice wall/bottom of the Upper Glacier is at 6000 m (19,685 ft),

with some campsites, and may take as many as 12 hours of climbing from the 5100-m (16,732-ft) campsite at the base of the Middle Glacier.

Traverse up and right across the 25- to 35-degree Upper Glacier, avoiding the seracs and crevasses, to the spur on the headwall of the South Face. This may take all day depending on whether one encounters fresh, deep snow (**avalanche danger**) or penitentes. Approach the spur from the left, and look for a way across the bergschrund. Once this is overcome, follow some ice ramps (50 to 55 degrees) up and right and climb onto the crest of the spur. The last good campsite is located here at 6500 m (21,325 ft), and this takes from 9 to 12 hours from the base of the Upper Glacier.

Ascend the crest to a pair of chimneys (to UIAA V; YDS 5.7), followed by a sharp ridge crest of 150 meters (500 feet) of mixed climbing (UIAA IV–V; YDS 5.5–5.7) that deadends against an unclimbable wall. Traverse to the right onto a 40- to 50-degree snow/ice slope, and then go straight up for 80 meters (260 feet) over 45- to 55-degree snow/ice slopes to the top of the South Face. Turn left and follow the gentle East Ridge to the summit.

MESSNER VARIATION OF THE FRENCH ROUTE

This has also been called the Messner Exit, the South Tyrolean Variation, and the Direct Variation. It was first climbed on January 23, 1974, by Reinhold Messner, who was part of an eight-person team. This has become the preferred variation of the French Route, as it is shorter than the other variations but presents essentially the same technical difficulties. On the other hand, this variation cannot be recommended with much recent snow (**avalanche danger**) nor with sparse snow (**rockfall danger**). The original French Route is a better choice under these conditions.

Instead of traversing up and right across the Upper Glacier, climb up and slightly left over 50- to 55-degree slopes, aiming for the prominent rock bottleneck that is to the left of the upper headwall. There is a gaping 'schrund beneath The Bottleneck and the rock is frequently verglassed. This is overcome by climbing up and left for five or six pitches (to UIAA V; YDS 5.7) across The Bottleneck, and continuing left onto the next snowslope. Make a direct ascent of the 50-degree snowslope, keeping to the right of a serac and left of a small rock cliff. This is

followed by snowslopes of 30 to 40 degrees that lead to the Cresta del Guanaco. Turn right (east) on the ridge crest, and follow it to the North Summit.

JAPANESE VARIATION OF THE FRENCH ROUTE

This variation to the French Route climbs the wall of rotten rock that is to the right of the upper spur. It was first climbed on January 29, 1981, by Masayoshi Yamamoto and Hironobu Kamuro.

SLOVENE VARIATION OF THE FRENCH ROUTE

This variation ascends the left side of the toe of the central buttress, meeting the French Route at the base of the Great Towers. It avoids the rockfall that may occur on the original French Route. It was first climbed on January 22, 1982, by Milan Crnilogar, Igor Skamperle, Slavko Sveticic, and Bogdan Biscak.

From the left (west) side of the central buttress, begin by climbing the right side of the Great Couloir, skirting a large crevasse on the left. Move to the right and climb up the left side of the buttress, over easy snow slopes and small rock steps (UIAA III; YDS 5.4), to the crest of the central buttress and the foot of the Great Towers.

LOWER ARGENTINE VARIATION OF THE FRENCH ROUTE

This variation was climbed by Gustavo and Daniel Pizarro in February 1992. Begin by climbing the lower slope of the Lower Glacier, up and left, to the base of the broad chute that marks the lower central buttress. Continue straight up the broad chute, over bad rock, to the crest of the central buttress and the foot of the Great Towers.

UPPER ARGENTINE VARIATION OF THE FRENCH ROUTE

This variation to the Messner Variation was also climbed in February 1992 by Daniel and Gustavo Pizarro. Go up and right above The Bottleneck and climb a small spur (UIAA V+; YDS 5.8) that leads to the Cresta del Guanaco. This spur ends atop the ridge very close to where the Canaleta of the Normal Route meets the Cresta del Guanaco.

LA RULETA RUSA

This route makes a direct ascent of the Lower and Middle Glaciers on the South Face of Aconcagua. The name of this route means "Russian roulette" in Spanish, in recognition of the avalanches that routinely sweep down it and the falling chunks of ice from the Middle Glacier. Among my friends, I call it "Avalanche Alley," and I cannot recommend this route due to its perilous nature. It was first climbed in 1988 by Slavko Sveticic and Milan Romih.

Begin by making a direct ascent of the Lower Glacier, aiming for the subtle 70-degree couloir in the middle of the glacier. This couloir flattens out to 45 degrees beneath the 90-degree cliff. Surmount the cliff directly, followed by a 40-degree chute, and then make a left diagonal traverse to the left side of the headwall at the top of the Lower Glacier. There are four couloirs on the left side of the headwall. Climb the second couloir from left. The lower third of this couloir is 60 degrees, and the middle third approaches 80 degrees. Leave the couloir about two-thirds of the way up, and traverse up and right over UIAA V + (YDS 5.8) rock to the bottom of the Central Glacier. Overcoming this vertical–to-overhanging ice cliff is the crux of the route. Once this is overcome, ascend the 30- to 40-degree slopes of the Central Glacier to its headwall, and then traverse left to the French Route.

CENTRAL ROUTE

This route is also called the Argentine–Austrian Route and the Fonrouge–Schönberger Route. It was first climbed in alpine style over a period of 4 days on February 9, 1966, by José Luis Fonrouge and Hans Schönberger. This is probably the technically easiest route on the South Face of Aconcagua, but as with La Ruleta Rusa, it is exposed to the danger of falling ice and avalanches, and cannot be recommended.

The route begins on the far right-hand side of the Lower Glacier and climbs up and left beneath a cliff with prominent frozen waterfalls. At the left-hand edge of the "waterfall cliff," climb a short couloir to a ramp that leads up and left to the seracs of the Middle Glacier. Bypass the seracs by climbing the far right-hand side of the Middle Glacier. Once above the seracs, traverse left across the Middle Glacier to meet the French Route.

FRENCH DIRECT ROUTE

This route was first climbed on February 11, 1985, after a two-week siege by Jean Paul Chassagne, Pierre Raveneau, Jean-Marcel Dufour, and Bernard Vallet, who were part of a seven-member expedition. It climbs a buttress on the rock cliff with frozen waterfalls that is to the right of the Central Route.

Begin by ascending the right side of the Lower Glacier to the bottom of the three shallow rock ribs beneath the buttress. Pass these on their left side and climb to the top of the ribs, where the first ascent party had a campsite (4700 m; 15,420 ft). The real climbing starts on the left side of the prow of the buttress, up an obtuse chute for four pitches (nothing harder than UIAA IV +; YDS 5.6) to a ledge. This ledge leads to the right to the narrow snow couloir behind the buttress. Climb the couloir for three pitches to the broad snowfield at the top of the buttress; this snowfield is fed by three couloirs, and the first ascent party named this feature The Spider. Climb the left couloir for one pitch, and then go left and up (UIAA V; YDS 5.7) across a rock wall. The next pitch continues up and left with some easy aid climbing, before going up and right (UIAA IV; YDS 5.5) to end on the crest of a small ridge that overlooks a couloir. The fourteenth pitch follows the crest of the ridge upward (UIAA III; YDS 5.4) to the next campsite, at the foot of the small glacier above (5100 m; 16,732 ft).

Lower Horcones Glacier

The route continues up and right across this small glacier to the next glacier to the right, which I call the Pasic Glacier (also known as the Lower East Glacier; the eastern lobe of this glacier actually drops

into the Relinchos Valley on the east side of Aconcagua). The French Direct Route meets the Argentine Route at approximately 6100 m (20,000 ft) on the Lower East Glacier.

ARGENTINE ROUTE

This route is also called the Pasic Route. It ascends the right-hand side of the South Face before traversing left to meet the French Route. It was first climbed on February 2, 1966, by Omar Pellergrini and Jorge Aikes, who were part of an Argentine team with Jean Pierre Demay and Willy Noll. This expedition spent four weeks establishing this route after an attempt during the previous year.

Begin by climbing a penitente slope that is beneath a hanging glacier on the right side of the South Face. The first ascent party established their first camp along this slope at an altitude of 4800 m (15,748 ft). A steep chute above this campsite leads to a frozen waterfall that drops from the Pasic Glacier. Climb this waterfall to the glacier, where the first ascent party had a camp at 5400 m (17,716 ft). Traverse left and up across the Pasic Glacier to its left edge (campsite at 6000 m; 19,685 ft), and climb up and over the vertical seracs that loom overhead until reaching the middle of the Upper Glacier, where the first ascent party established their fourth camp at approximately 6400 m (21,000 ft). From this camp on the Upper Glacier, climb onto the spur on the headwall of the South Face, and continue to the summit via the French Route.

SLOVENE 1986 ROUTE

This could be considered a variation of either the Argentine or French Direct routes. It was first climbed on February 23, 1986, by Danilo Tic and Milan Romih, after having spent 6 days climbing the French Direct Route. It starts above the seracs on the Upper Glacier by ascending a snow/ice couloir, with sections up to 90 degrees and UIAA VI (YDS 5.9), to the crest of the East Ridge. Follow the crest of the upper East Ridge (described in the next chapter under the East Glacier Route) to the summit.

Chapter Five

VACAS AND RELINCHOS VALLEYS APPROACH

The trailhead for this approach is at Punta de Vacas, a small settlement located along Highway 7, approximately 166 kilometers (103 miles) from the city of Mendoza. There is a large Gendarmeria (the Argentine border patrol) station here and a bus stop. Most climbers who approach Aconcagua via the Vacas and Relinchos Valleys stay at Los Penitentes or Puente del Inca.

From Punta de Vacas (2325 m, 7,628 ft; 32° 51' 00"S, 69° 45' 36"W) hike up the west (left) side of the Río de las Vacas to the primitive La Leña shelter (2700 m; 8,858 ft). This is an 11.8-kilometer (7-mile) hike, and takes about 4 hours from Punta de Vacas. This is where the Aconcagua Provincial Park rangers examine permits and issue rubbish bags. Many parties elect to camp here, taking a more leisurely 3 days to approach Plaza Argentina. There is a seasonal, temporary bridge across the Río de las Vacas about 0.3 km (0.2 mi) upstream from the La Leña shelter. If the bridge is missing, then it is best to cross the swift and deep river on horseback. The best crossing may be slightly downstream from the shelter, where the river is shallow and wide.

Continue hiking up the Río de las Vacas to the Casa de Piedra shelter (3200 m, 10,500 ft; 32° 37' 54"S, 69° 50' 24"W), located along the east bank of the river, directly opposite the steep and narrow Relinchos Valley. This is a 13.7-kilometer (8.2-mile) hike from the La Leña shelter, and takes about 5 to 6 hours of hiking. The Casa de Piedra is the usual campsite used during the hike-in. As with the La Leña shelter, the primitive stone hut has no facilities, except for a roof, fireplace, grill, and rock windbreaks that serve as tent or bivouac sites. Potable water can be obtained from a spring to the north of the hut. The spring is marked by a meadow, and it is advisable to take the water that comes directly out of the spring. Horses and mules are usually staked out in the meadow. The hut is frequently occupied by Gendarmeria patrols.

The Polish Glacier

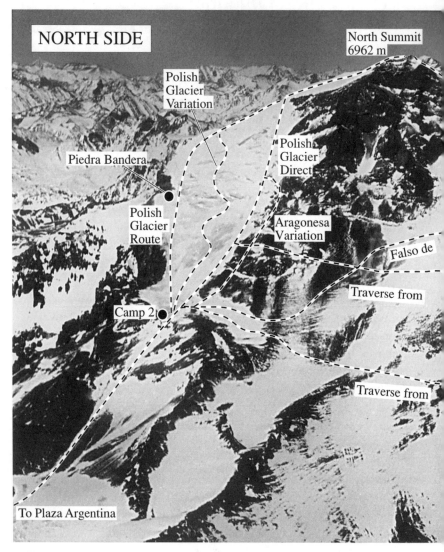

Photo by Albert W. Stevens, © National Geographic Society

Punta de Vacas

La Leña shelter

(The Gendarmeria is Argentina's border patrol. It is not the same as the army, but could be compared to a paramilitary force, such as the Royal Canadian Mounted Police. Unlike the Border Patrol in the United States, the Gendarmeria is more likely to be looking for smugglers than illegal immigrants. The most popular smuggled goods in the mid-1980s were electronics and booze, and Gendarmeria horse and mule patrols were looking for illicit pack trains from Chile loaded with scotch and video cassette recorders. The few patrols I have met have been professional and courteous. They may ask to see your permit and passports, and may even invite you to dinner!)

From Casa de Piedra, hike up the Relinchos Valley. The Relinchos Valley is directly opposite Casa de Piedra, across the Río de las Vacas. Cross the river upstream from the Relinchos. The crossing is relatively easy, but it is much easier on horseback.

Crossing the Relinchos River

The Relinchos starts out as a steep, narrow canyon with a good use trail on its right (north) side. It may be necessary to cross the rushing stream a few times before coming out at the hanging valley above. Follow the south side of the stream up the flat, hanging valley to the moraines that mark Plaza Argentina (4200 m, 13,780 ft, 32° 38' 48"S, 69° 56' 42"W). This 10-kilometer (6-mile) hike takes 6 hours from Casa de Piedra. Plaza Argentina is the usual base camp for the East Glacier and Polish Glacier routes on Aconcagua. A park ranger is stationed here throughout the climbing season, and has radio contact with other park rangers and outfitters. The campsites are in the moraine, with many sites for tents located in rock windbreaks. The moraine is actually a rock-covered glacier. Water can be obtained from pools of ice on the surface of the glacier; these aren't very obvious, and it is necessary to hunt for them.

There are two other approaches to the Polish Glacier. The first continues up the Vacas Valley and continues around the north and west sides of Ameghino to the southern branch of the Vacas Glacier. Continue up the glacier to the base of the Polish Glacier (at 5900 m; 19,350 ft). This alternative is much longer, but it passes through a much wilder area.

Aconcagua and Ameghino from the Relinchos Valley

View north from Polish Glacier Route; Mercedario in distance

The other approach avoids the Vacas and Relinchos Valleys completely, and instead follows the Horcones Valley approach and the Normal Route as far as Nido de Cóndores. Leave the Normal Route here and at first make a slightly descending traverse to the east before moving up and left (southeast) to the base of the Polish Glacier (at 5900 m; 19,350 ft). The Polish Glacier can also be approached from the Berlin Camp. Follow the Normal Route from Berlin to a point beyond the White Rocks campsite. Traverse to the east (left) across the gentle north slope of Aconcagua to the right side of the Polish Glacier where there are some campsites at 6100 m (20,100 ft); a few cliffs must be negotiated on this higher traverse, but these shouldn't be more difficult than class 2 on the Yosemite Decimal System.

Conversely, it is also possible (and very common) to approach the upper part of the Normal Route from the Polish Glacier campsite at 5900 m (19,350 ft). This is described below under the Falso de los Polacos route.

SOUTHEAST RIDGE ROUTE

Technically speaking, there is no Southeast Ridge on Aconcagua. This route, in reality, approaches the East Ridge of Aconcagua from the southeast, by way of the Relinchos Valley. It was first climbed February 24, 1966, by Rolf Röcker, Othmar Horak, and Dieter Sause. Head southwest from Plaza Argentina, crossing many tedious fields of scree, penitentes, and moraine, and climb onto the Pasic Glacier. From this glacier, gain the crest of the East Ridge of Aconcagua, and follow it to where the difficulties increase dramatically above the East Glacier. The rest of the route is described under the East Glacier Route, below.

This route was approached from Plaza Francia (the usual base camp site for routes on the South Face) in 1990 by Mauricio Fernández and Carlos Domínguez. They crossed Portezuelo Relinchos (5100 m; 16,732 ft) before climbing onto the glacier.

EAST GLACIER ROUTE

This route is also known as the English Glacier and the Argentine Route. It was first attempted by a British expedition (hence the name), but first climbed by Argentines Guillermo Vieiro, Edgardo Porcelana, and Jorge Víctor Jasson on January 27, 1978. This route ascends the East Glacier of Aconcagua, formed by the cirque between the eastern cliffs of the Polish Glacier and the lower East Ridge.

Head northwest from Plaza Argentina across the moraines of the Relinchos Glacier (along the first part of the Polish Glacier Route) to the campsite located beneath the prominent field of penitentes. Instead of climbing to the right onto the penitentes, turn left, and ascend the valley that leads to the East Glacier. The base of the glacier is at approximately 4900 m (16,075 ft), where there is a campsite. Climb up onto the lower glacier by means of an ice couloir/ledge that leads up and left, surrounded by a loose, rocky slope. There is a campsite above the couloir and at the bottom of the lower glacier.

The glacier is divided into three parts: lower, middle, and upper. The glacier consists of ice, soft snow, and some moderate penitentes. The most difficult section of the glacier is between the middle and upper parts: the angle is between 60 and 65 degrees in this area, and the ice

is the hardest. Move to the left side of the upper glacier, and climb a small, steep ridge to the gentle ridge that marks the top of the glacier (6200 m; 20,340 ft); the 1986 Yugoslav Variation on the South Face ends here, as does the misnamed Southeast Ridge. There are several good campsites along this ridge.

View of the South Face of Aconcagua from the East Ridge

Follow the ridge to the base of the wall, where the real technical challenges begin. This 200-meter (660-foot) step is the crux of the route, with mixed climbing from UIAA IV to VI (YDS 5.5 to 5.9). It is very exposed and especially loose, anchors are scarce, and solid hand- or footholds are almost impossible to find. The step is followed by a short ice couloir, which leads to a small snowfield, the only practical campsite on this section of the route. Traverse to the right across the snowfield and climb an almost vertical ice couloir. This is followed by patchy snow slopes covering loose scree to the crest of the East Ridge of Aconcagua. Follow the upper East Ridge (the upper part of the Polish Glacier Route) to the summit.

POLISH GLACIER ROUTE

The first ascent was made March 8, 1934, by Konstanty Narkievitcz-Jodko, Stefan Daszyinski, Wictor Ostrowski, and Stefan Osiecki. This route ascends the prominent glacier on the northeast slope of the mountain. It is the second most popular route on Aconcagua, and its aesthetic nature makes it the preferred route for climbers with moderate experience. Ice axes, crampons, and full crevasse rescue equipment will be needed.

Several trails lead northwest from Plaza Argentina over the moraine of the Relinchos Glacier. These trails are marked by cairns, and it is usually easier to follow the cairns rather than a specific trail. After following the cairns over the rubble, one arrives at a campsite near the bottom of a steep slope, marked by high cliffs to the left and a field of penitentes to the right. The penitentes are surrounded by slopes of scree, and most parties find it easier to ascend through the penitentes (still hard work) and, while descending, take advantage of the scree slope to the left. From the top of the field of penitentes, move left and cross a

small stream to a campsite beneath some large rocks. This is the usual site of Camp 1 (5000 m; 16,400 ft) and takes about 4 hours from Plaza Argentina. This is the only campsite on the Polish Glacier Route that features running water during the afternoon thaw.

From Camp 1, some parties make their next camp atop Ameghino Col (5380 m; 17,650 ft), the pass between Ameghino and Aconcagua. Ameghino Col is usually bypassed, however, and most parties continue climbing up the slope to the left that leads to the base of the Polish Glacier itself. There is a small campsite at 5700 m (18,700 ft) and another larger campsite at 5900 m (19,350 ft; 32° 38' 07"S, 69° 58' 36"W), the usual site for Camp 2, about 6 hours from Camp 1. Camp 2 is right up against the cliffs, just below the lower level of the Polish Glacier. It is a small site, with room for only eight tents, at the most. There are some other campsites further to the right of the cliffs, in a flat area below the glacier. Most parties use these sites as their high camp and climb to the summit in a long day from here.

From the "cliff camp," traverse to the right and climb onto the glacier. The lower part of the Polish Glacier is flat, and usually consists of penitentes. Force your way through these obstacles, and then make a diagonal ascending traverse to the left (30 to 35 degrees), aiming for the Piedra Bandera, the prominent dark rock with a large white band in its middle. (It bears a loose resemblance to the Argentine national flag.) There are campsites at the base of Piedra Bandera (6400 m; 20,997 ft).

Pass the Piedra Bandera on its right side, but keep to the left of the seracs in the middle of the glacier; this area is known as The Bottleneck (40 degrees). Continue climbing up the 30- to 35-degree left side of the glacier above the Piedra Bandera, avoiding the seracs in the middle of the glacier, and use caution to avoid crevasses. Climb to the crest of the East Ridge of Aconcagua, and follow the ridge (with too many false summits) to the top.

There are many variations to the Polish Glacier Route, and perhaps the most common one is to climb the middle portion of the glacier, zigzagging among the seracs (with angles of 45 degrees or so) before climbing onto the East Ridge of Aconcagua. While this variation is more difficult and slightly more hazardous (due to the seracs and crevasses) than The Bottleneck, the snow conditions in the middle portion of the glacier may be better for climbing.

Approach to Camp 1, Polish Glacier Route

Approaching Camp 2, Polish Glacier Route

Camp 2 (5900 m; 19,357 ft), Polish Glacier Route

POLISH GLACIER DIRECT ROUTE

This route is also known as the "Argentine Finish," "Argentine Variation," and the "Tucumán Variation." It was first climbed in 1961 by Orlando Bravo, Tato Bellomio, and Dado Liebich, members of the Club Andino Tucumán in Argentina. Instead of climbing the left side of the Polish Glacier, this route climbs its right side. There are some campsites beyond the right side of the glacier at 6100 m (20,100 ft). Keep to the right of the seracs in the middle of the glacier, but stay left of the cliffs that mark the north face of Aconcagua. The angle varies from 45 to 50 degrees for a short stretch at approximately 6500 m (21,325 ft), and then decreases dramatically. The upper slopes lead to the crest of the East Ridge of Aconcagua. Follow the ridge to the summit.

ARAGONESA VARIATION OF THE POLISH GLACIER DIRECT ROUTE

This variation to the Polish Glacier Direct Route was climbed on January 18, 1995, by Javier Alvira, José Antonio Hidalgo, José Vilalta, and Javier

Subías. Leave the right side of the Polish Glacier at approximately 6000 m (19,684 ft) and climb a series of chutes and couloirs, with rock steps up to UIAA IV+ (YDS 5.6) and maximum angle of 75-degree snow/ice. These lead to a long ramp that leads left to meet the Polish Glacier Direct Route at 6500 m (21,325 ft).

FALSO DE LOS POLACOS

Many expeditions do the Vacas and Relinchos Valleys approach and climb Aconcagua via the Normal Route, either by design (to avoid the crowds at Plaza de Mulas) or last-minute decision (due to weather, snow conditions on the Polish Glacier, or lack of skills and strength). This is accomplished by making a diagonal traverse up and to the right from the 5900-m (19,356-ft) cliff camp at the base of the Polish Glacier. The very bottom, flat part of the Polish Glacier must be crossed before moving onto the scree fields that mark the north side of Aconcagua. Keep well to the left of the Northwest Ridge until it is possible to traverse to the right onto the ridge crest, meeting the Normal Route at approximately 6300 m (20,670 ft), a point beneath the Independencia hut and above

View of Pacific Ocean from 6100 m (20,012 ft) on the Polish Glacier Route

Climbing the Polish Glacier; Piedra Bandera in distance

Climbing the Polish Glacier

Penitentes on Ameghino Glacier, Polish Glacier Route

the White Rocks campsite. Continue up the Normal Route and the Canaleta from there.

Also, many Polish Glacier climbers elect to descend the Normal Route. One can leave the Normal Route anywhere between the Independencia hut and the White Rocks campsite and head northeast and down to the base of the Polish Glacier. This is as easy as it sounds, and it takes about 4 hours to descend to the base of the Polish Glacier from the summit via this route.

NORTH FACE ROUTE

This route was first climbed on January 27, 1986, by Claudio Schranz from the Berlin Camp. Two days previously, he and his partner, Mauro Ferrari, had climbed the Polish Glacier Route in a day from the Berlin Camp.

The north side of the summit of Aconcagua is marked by cliffs and pinnacles, divided by some gullies. Schranz said that this route is not technically difficult, but route-finding among the pinnacles and gullies was a problem.

Appendix A
FURTHER READING

BOOKS

Aconcagua: El Centinela de Piedra; The Sentinel of Stone (1991), by Alejandro Randis and María Marta Lavoisier. Randis–Lavoisier, C.C. 319, 5500 Mendoza, Argentina. This is a large-format "coffee table" book, written by an experienced Aconcagua guide from Mendoza. All of the major routes are outlined, in addition to discussions on wildlife, geology, glaciology, and climate. The authoritative text (in Spanish and English) is enhanced by the striking art of Ms. Lavoisier.

2000 South American Handbook. Passport Books, 4225 West Touhy Avenue, Lincolnwood, IL 60646-1975. This annual publication changes editors every year, and the first word of its title is the year. This essential guidebook is immorally expensive, but it covers the entire continent of South America with an incredible amount of accurate detail.

Aconcagua—The Stone Sentinel; Perspectives of an Expedition (1992), by Thomas E. Taplin. Eli Ely Publishers, P.O. Box 5245, Santa Monica, CA 90409-5245. This entertaining book describes an ascent of the Normal Route by a commercial, guided expedition, told from the perspective of each client. It features intra-family rivalries, petty arguments, budding love affairs, accidents, rescues, success, and failure.

WEB SITES

Aconcagua Provincial Park. http://www.aconcagua.mendoza.gov.ar/ (in Spanish and English)

Mount Aconcagua—Unofficial Home Page. http://www.mt-aconcagua.com (in Spanish only)

Aconcagua: The Professional Site. http://www.aconcagua.com (in English, Spanish, and Italian)

Appendix B
EQUIPMENT LIST

CLOTHING

hiking socks with liners (two pairs)
hiking boots
cold-weather socks with liners (three pairs)
plastic bags (as vapor barrier liners for socks)
lightweight long underwear, tops and bottoms
"expedition-weight" long underwear, tops and bottoms
pile jacket
pile trousers
pile balaclava
windbreaker, waterproof/breathable
wind pants, waterproof/breathable
synthetic parka with hood
warm cap
neck gaiter
glove liners
wool mittens
overmitts
gaiters
sun hat
short trousers
T-shirts
sunglasses
old tennis shoes for river crossings

CAMPING EQUIPMENT

knapsack
duffel bag, with lock
sunscreen

lip balm
three one-liter water bottles
compass
altimeter
pocket knife
first-aid kit
toothbrush, toothpaste, soap
four-season tent
sleeping bag
two foam pads
cup and spoon
headlamp
cigarette lighter
gasoline stove
three one-liter fuel bottles
cooking pot
water-purification supplies

CLIMBING EQUIPMENT

All Routes:
double mountaineering boots
ice axe
crampons
Add for Polish Glacier:
prusiks
50 meters of 9-millimeter rope
harness
ice screws, pickets, and/or deadmen
pulleys
carabiners
runners
Add for Technical Routes:
helmet
chocks
rock pitons
aiders

MORE GOOD STUFF
notebooks, pens, pencils
Spanish-English dictionary
roadmaps and topographical maps
guidebooks
two cameras (one for color, one for black and white)
color and black-and-white film
plastic bags (to repackage food)

Appendix C
BOOKKEEPING

Many expedition treasurers do an excellent job of fouling up their books. This results in an unfair financial burden on some, while others in the same party seem to enjoy a free holiday in the mountains. The following system has been used with great success by many expeditions. It is adapted from the method described by Boyd N. Everett, Jr., in his seminal essay, *The Organization of an Alaskan Expedition*.[16]

The treasurer must keep two sets of records: Expenses Paid and Cash Transactions. Expenses Paid are group expenses that have been paid to others who are not part of the expedition. Cash Transactions are payments made between members of the expedition, and this category includes advances made to the treasurer by the members and loans between members. For example, one member may go to the post office and buy stamps for another member. This Cash Transaction would be a Loan, and not Expenses Paid to another party, as this was not a group expense. This is the most common error made by treasurers: confusing Cash Transactions with Expenses Paid. Here is a sample statement for a four-person expedition:

Expenses Paid	John	Paul	George	Ringo	Total
Mules	309				309
Bus Tickets		31	16		47
Taxis		8	3		11
Fuel	10				10
Lodging		73			73
Meals		69	79		148
Tips	4		18		22
Total	323	181	116	0	620

Expenses per person: $620 divided by 4 = $155

Cash Transactions	John	Paul	George	Ringo
Advances	(143)		43	100
Loan	(3)	3		
Total	(146)	3	43	100

Reconciliation of Accounts	John	Paul	George	Ringo
Expenses Paid	323	181	116	0
Cash Transactions	(146)	3	43	100
Net Paid	177	184	159	100
Expenses per Person	(155)	(155)	(155)	(155)
Net	22	29	4	(55)

Ringo owes the other members of the expedition a total of $55. John, as treasurer, would collect $55 from Ringo, and pay Paul $29, George $4, and himself $22.

OUTFITTERS AND GUIDES

Argentina's telephone country code is 54, and Mendoza's area code is 261. One must dial a "0" before the area code when dialing long distance within Argentina.

Aymará Turismo y Aventura
9 de Julio 1023
5500 Mendoza
Telephone and fax: 54-261-420-0607, 54-261-420-5304, 54-261-420-2064, 54-261-423-0433
e-mail: info@aymara.com.ar
web site: http://www.aymara.com.ar
Services: Mules, ground transportation, porters, rooms and meals at the Hotel Refugio near Plaza de Mulas.

Campo Base Adventures and Expeditions
Mitre 946
5500 Mendoza
Telephone: 54-261-429-0707
e-mail: info@campobase.com.ar
web site: http://www.campo-base.com.ar
Services: Hostel in Mendoza, transport to Puente del Inca, mules, guides, porters, camps at Confluencia and Plaza de Mulas.

Aconcagua Trek
Guiraldes 246
5519 Dorrego, Mendoza
Telephone and fax: 54-261-431-7003
e-mail: rudy@lanet.com.ar; aconcagua@rudyparra.com
web site: http://www.rudyparra.com
Services: Camping near Puente del Inca at Los Puquios, ground trans-

portation, mules, and base camp meals at Plaza de Mulas, Plaza Argentina, and Plaza Francia.

Fernando Grajales
José Federico Moreno 898, 6° B
5500 Mendoza
Telephone: 54-261-429-3830
e-mail: expediciones@grajales.net
web site: http://grajales.net
Services: Mules, guides, assistance in Mendoza, ground transportation, base camp meals at Plaza de Mulas. Grajales and his associates are based at Hotel Ayelen at Los Penitentes ski area from December until March.

Daniel Alessio
Casilla de Correos 33
5505 Mendoza
Fax: 54-261-496-2201
e-mail: aconcagua@alessio.com.ar
web site: http://www.alessio.com.ar
Services: Guides, mules, and base camp service at Plaza de Mulas and Plaza Argentina.

Aconcagua Express
Casilla 187 Correo 20
Santiago, Chile
Telephone (USA toll-free): 866-690-8423; Chile: 056-2-217-9101, 56-2-217-5017; Argentina: 54-261-510-7822. Fax: 56-2-215-1243
e-mail: adventure@kladventure.com
web site: www.kladventure.com
Services: Mules, ground transportation, satellite communications and base camp meals at Plaza de Mulas. This outfitter is based at Los Penitentes ski area.

David Vela
Andesport
Casilla de Correo 646

5500 Mendoza

Telephone and fax: 54-261-424-3782, 54-261-423-5992

e-mail: andesport@usa.net

Services: Mules, guides, base camp meals at Plaza de Mulas and Plaza Argentina, lodging and meals at the Penitentes Hostel at Los Penitentes ski area, ground transportation.

Inka Expeditions

Pedernera 2420

5547 Godoy Cruz, Mendoza

Telephone and fax: 54-261-428-2052

e-mail: inka@aconcagua.org.ar

web site: http://www.aconcagua.org.ar

Services: Guided expeditions, mules, base camp services at Plaza de Mulas and Plaza de Argentina.

Casa Orviz Mountain Shop

Juan B. Justo 536

5500 Mendoza

Telephone and fax: 54-261-425-1281

web site: http://www. orviz.com

Services: Sale and rental of climbing equipment, four-wheel drive ground transportation, general information.

Gabriel Cabrera

Rumbo al Horizonte Expediciones y Aventuras

Caseros 1053

M5501KDK Godoy Cruz, Mendoza

Telephone and fax: 54-261-452-0641

e-mail: info@rah.com.ar

web site: http://www.rumboalhorizonte.com.ar

Services: Complete guided expeditions.

Appendix E
SPEAKING SPANISH

PRONUNCIATION GUIDE

Argentine Spanish is a different language than the language spoken in Mexico or Spain. The Argentine dialect has a strong Italian accent, uses a lot of slang (almost as much as American English), and many exotic Castilian words.

When used before the Spanish letters *e* and *i*, the Spanish *c* is pronounced like the English *s*. For example, *el glaciar* (the glacier) is pronounced *el gla-see-AR*; *la cima* (the summit) is pronounced *la SEE-ma*. In all other cases, *c* is pronounced hard, like the English *k*.

Before the Spanish letters *e* and *i*, *g* is pronounced like the English *h*; in all other cases it is pronounced hard, like the English *g* in "good." For example, *el refugio* (the hut) is pronounced *el ray-FOO-hee-oh* and *el albergue* (the hut) is pronounced *el al-BER-gay*.

In Spanish, *h* is never pronounced. *Helar* (to freeze), for example, is pronounced *ay-LAR*.

The Spanish *j* is pronounced like the English *h*. *La Joya* (the jewel), for example, is pronounced *la HO-ya*.

The Spanish consonant *ll* is usually pronounced like the English *y*, as in *llano* (plain), pronounced *YA-no*.

The Spanish *y* is pronounced like the *y* in *yet*, never as the *y* in *only*. For example, *la joya* is pronounced *la HO-ya*.

The *ñ* in Spanish is similar to the *ny* in *canyon*. For example, *la cañada* (the ravine) is pronounced *la can-YA-da*.

The group of letters *que* is pronounced as *kay*.

The Spanish *z* is always pronounced like the English *s*. *Los zapatos* (the shoes) is pronounced *los sa-PAH-toes*.

VOCABULARY

Please note that the following words are in common use in Chile and Argentina, where the mountaineering vocabulary has its origins in the German language. Other Spanish-speaking countries (such as Mexico or Spain) more commonly use climbing words that are French in origiñ. So, an ice axe in Mexico is a *piolet* while in Argentina it is a *piqueta*. Please keep this in mind when using this vocabulary in other Spanish-speaking countries.

English	Spanish	Pronunciation
the abyss	el abismo	ah-BEES-mo
alpinism	andinismo	an-dee-NEES-mo
the alpinist	el andinista	an-dee-NEES-ta (masculine)
	la andinista	an-dee-NEES-ta (feminine)
the altitude sickness	la puna	POO-na
	la apunamiento	ah-poo-na-mee-EN-toe
the arête	la arista	ah-REES-ta
to arrive	llegar	yay-GAR
(at the summit)	(a la cumbre)	(ah la KOOM-bray)
the ascent	la subida	soo-BEE-da
the avalanche	el alud	ah-LOOD
	la avalancha	ah-va-LAN-cha
the bargaining	el regateo	ray-ga-TAY-o
the belay	el asegurado	ah-say-goo-RAH-doe
	el amarrado	ah-ma-RAH-doe
to belay	asegurar (to secure)	ah-say-goo-RAR
	amarrar (to anchor)	ah-ma-RAR
the bergschrund	la rimaya	reem-AY-ah
the bindings	las ataduras	sah-tah-DOO-ras
the bivouac	el vivaque	vee-VAH-kay
the blizzard	la ventisca	ven-TEES-ka
the bolt	la pitonisa	pee-ton-EE-sa
the boots	las botas	BO-tahs
(double)	(dobles)	(DOW-blays)
the bowline	la amarra de proa	ah-MA-rah day PRO-ah
the buttress	el contrafuerte	kon-trah-fu-AIR-tay
the cairn	la pirca	peer-KAH
the camp	el campamento	kam-pa-MEN-to
(high)	(alto)	(AL-to)

the candle	*la vela*	VAY-la
the cap	*el gorro*	GO-ro
the carabiners	*los mosquetones*	mos-kay-TONE-ays
the cartridge	*el cartucho*	kar-TOO-cho
the butane cartridge	*el cartucho de gas*	kar-TOO-cho day gas
	butano	boo-TAWN-oh
the chimney	*la chimenea*	chee-may-NAY-a
to chimney up	*deshollinar*	day-so-yee-NAR
the chock	*el empotrador*	em-po-TRA-dor
	el malacate	mal-ah-CAH-tay
	la cuña	KOON-nya
the cirque	*el circo*	SEER-KOH
the climb	*la subida*	soo-BEE-dah
to climb	*subir*	soo-BEER
the climber	*el escalador*	es-ka-la-DOR (masculine)
	la escaladora	es-ka-la-DOR-ah (feminine)
the cloud	*la nube*	NOO-bay
the col	*el cuello*	KWAY-yo
the compass	*el compás*	coam-PAS
	el ámbito	AM-bee-toe
	la brújula	BRU-hoo-la
the cornice	*la cornisa*	kor-NEE-sa
the couloir	*la canaleta*	can-al-AY-ta
the crack	*la hendidura*	en-dee-DOO-rah
the crampons	*los crampones*	kram-PON-ays
the crevasse	*la grieta*	gree-AY-ta
danger	*peligro*	pay-LEE-gro
the descender	*el ocho de descenso*	oh-cho day days-SEN-so
the descent	*la bajada*	bah-HA-da
the dihedral	*el diedro*	dee-AY-dro
east	*este, oriente*	ES-tay, o-ree-EN-tay
the etrier	*la escalilla*	es-ca-LEE-ya
exposed	*expuesto*	eks-PWAY-sto
the flashlight	*la linterna*	leen-TAIR-na
	eléctrica	ay-LEK-tree-ka
flat	*llano*	YA-no
the foam pad	*el colchón de esponja*	kol-CHON day ays-PON-ha
the fog	*la niebla*	nee-ABE-la

the food (provisions)	los comestibles	ko-mays-TEE-blays
frozen	congelado	kon-hay-LAD-oh
the front points	los clavos delantero	KLA-vos day-lan-TAY-row
the gaiters	las polainas	po-LA-ee-nas
the gasoline	la gasolina	gas-o-LEEN-a
(white)	la bencina	ben-SEE-na
	blanca	BLAN-ka
	la nafta	NAFF-ta
the glacier	el glaciar	gla-see-AR
	el ventisquero	ven-tees-KAY-row
the gloves	los guantes	GWAN-tays
the goggles	el visor	VEE-sor
the guide	el guía	GEE-ah
the hammer	el martillo	mar-TEE-yo
the hardware store	la ferretería	fay-ray-tay-REE-ah
the harness	el arnés	ar-NAYS
	el cinturón	seen-too-ROWN
the headlamp	la lámpara de la cabeza	LAM-par-ah day la ca-BAY-sa
	la linterna frontal	leen-TAYR-na FRON-tal
the headwall	la placa	PLA-kah
height	altura	al-TOO-ra
the helmet	el casco	KAS-ko
HELP!	¡SOCORRO!	so-KO-ro
high	alto	AL-to
the highway	la carretera	ka-ray-TAIR-ah
the hut	el refugio	ray-FOO-he-o
	la cabaña	ka-BAN-ya
	el albergue	al-BAIR-gay
the ice	el hielo	ee-AY-lo
the ice axe	la piqueta	pee-KAY-ta
	el piolet	pee-OH-lay
the ice field	la zona de helado	SON-ah day ay-LAD-oh
the ice hammer	el martillo para hielo	mar-TEE-yo PAH-rah ee-AY-lo
the ice screw	el tornillo de hielo	tor-NEE-yo day ee-AY-lo
icy	helado	ay-LAD-oh
the jacket	la chaqueta	cha-KAY-ta
(down)	(de plumón)	(day ploo-MONE)
the inner boot	la bota interior	BOW-tah een-tay-REE-or

to jump	*saltar*	sal-TAR
the kerosene	*la kerosena*	kair-oh-SAIN-ah
	el petróleo	pay-TRO-lay-o
the knife	*el cuchillo*	koo-CHEE-yo
(pocket)	*(de bolsillo)*	(day bol-SEE-yo)
the knot	*el nudo*	NEW-doe
the lighter	*el encendedor*	en-sen-DAY-dor
the lightning	*el relámpago*	ray-LAM-paw-go
the map	*el mapa*	MA-pa
(topographic map)	*(carta topográfica)*	(toe-po-GRA-fee-ka)
the matches	*los fósforos*	FOS-fo-ros
the mittens	*los mitones*	mee-TONE-ays
the moraine	*el chancal*	CHAWN-call
the mountaineer	*el montañista*	mone-tonn-YEES-ta (masculine)
	el andinista	an-dee-NEES-ta (masculine)
	la montañista	mone-tonn-YEES-ta (feminine)
	la andinista	an-dee-NEES-ta (feminine)
mountaineering	*andinismo*	an-dee-NEES-mo
	montañismo	mone-tonn-YEES-mo
(equipment)	*(el equipo de andinismo)*	(ay-KEE-po day an-dee-NEES-mo)
the mountains	*las montañas*	mone-TONN-yas
(high)	*(altas)*	(AL-tas)
the mule driver	*el arriero*	ar-ree-AY-ro
north	*norte*	NOR-tay
the open book	*el libro abierto*	LEE-bro ah-bee-AIR-toe
the outer boot	*la contrafuerte*	cone-tra-FWAIR-tay
the overboots	*las cubrebotas*	koo-bray-BO-tas
the pack	*la mochila*	mo-CHEE-la
the pack animals	*las acémilas*	ah-SAY-mee-las
the pass	*el portezuelo*	por-tay-SWAY-lo
the peak	*el cerro*	SAY-row
	el pico	PEE-ko
	el picacho	pee-KA-cho
the pitons	*las pitones*	pee-TONE-ays
the plateau	*el altiplano*	al-tee-PLA-no
the porter	*el porteador*	por-tay-AH-dor
the precipice	*el precipicio*	pray-see-PEE-see-o
the pulley	*la polea*	po-LAY-ah

the rappel	*el rappel*	rap-PEL
the ravine	*la quebrada*	kay-BRAH-dah
	la cañada	kan-YA-da
to rent, charter	*alquiler*	al-kee-LAIR
	rentar	ren-TAR
	fletar	flay-TAR
the ridge	*el filo*	FEE-lo
the rime	*la escarcha*	es-KAR-cha
the road	*el camino*	ka-MEE-no
ROCK!	*¡PIEDRA!*	pee-AY-dra
the rock	*la piedra*	pee-AY-dra
	la roca	RO-ka
the rockfall	*la caída de piedra*	ka-EE-da day pee-AY-dra
the rocks	*el terreno*[17]	teh-RAY-no
(loose)	*(suelto)*	(SWEL-toe)
(solid)	*(sólido)*	(SO-lee-doe)
the rope	*la cuerda*	KWAIR-da
	la soga	SO-ga
the rope team	*la cordada*	kor-DA-da
the route	*la ruta*	ROO-ta
the sand	*la arena*	ah-RAY-na
the scree	*el aluvión*	ah-loo-vee-OWN
the shovel	*la pala*	PA-la
to ski	*esquiar*	es-kee-AR
(alpine)	*(alpino)*	(al-PEEN-oh)
(Nordic)	*(nórdico)*	(NOR-dee-koh)
the ski poles	*los bastones*	bas-TONE-ays
the skis	*los esquís*	es-KEES
the sled	*el trineo*	tree-NAY-oh
the sleeping bag	*la bolsa de dormir*	BOL-sa day dor-MEER
the slope	*la pendiente*	pen-dee-YEN-tay
the snow	*la nieve*	nee-AY-vay
(new)	*(reciente)*	(ray-see-EN-tay)
(powder)	*(polvorosa)*	(pol-vo-ROS-ah)
the snowbridge	*el puente de nieve*	PWEN-tay day nee-AY-vay
the snow anchor	*la fijador para nieve*	fee-HA-dor par-ah nee-AY-vay
("deadman")	*(hombre muerto)*	OM-bray MWAIR-to

the snow drift	la ventisca	ven-TEES-ka
south	sud, sur	sood, soor
the stake, peg	la estaca	es-TAH-kah
steep	escarpado	es-kar-PA-doe
STOP!	¡PARE!	PAR-ay
	¡párese!	PAR-ay-say
the stove	la estufa	es-TOO-fa
	la calentador	ka-len-ta-DOR
the straps	las cintas	SEEN-tahs
the stream	la corriente	ko-ree-EN-tay
the summit	la cumbre	KOOM-bray
	la cima	SEE-ma
the sunglasses	los lentes oscuros	LAIN-tays os-KOO-ros
the supergaiters	las super polainas	SOO-pair po-LA-ee-nas
the supermarket	el supermercado	soo-pair-mair-KAH-doe
the sweater	el suéter	SWAY-tair
the talus	el talud	ta-LOOD
the tent	la carpa	KAR-pa
the tent fly	el toldo	TOL-doe
the trail	el sendero	sen-DAY-ro
to traverse	atravesar	ah-tra-vay-SAR
the tumpline	la mecapal	may-CAP-al
the valley	la quebrada	kay-BRAH-dah
	el valle	VA-yay
the village	el pueblo	PWAY-blo
the (rock) wall	el muro	MOO-row
the (mud) wall	la tapia	TA-pee-ah
the water	el agua	AH-gwa
(purified)	(purificado)	(poo-ree-fee-KAH-doe)
the water bottle	la botella de agua	bo-TAY-ya day AH-gwa
	la cantimplora	can-teem-PLOR-ah
west	oeste, occidente	o-WES-tay, ok-see-DEN-tay
the wind	el viento	vee-EN-toe
the windbreaker	el rompeviento	rom-pay-vee-EN-toe
the wrist sling	la correa de muñeca	co-RAY-ah day moon-YAY-kah
to zigzag up	subir en zigzag	soo-BEER en zig-zag
the zipper	el cierre	see-YAY-ray

CLIMBING PHRASES

Continue straight ahead.
Siga adelante.

Turn right (left).
Da una vuelta a la derecha (izquierda).

How far is it to . . . ?
¿Como tan lejos está . . . ?

Can we get to . . . before dark?
¿Podemos llegar a . . . antes de la noche?

Crampons and ice axe are essential.
Son esenciales los crampones y la piqueta.

Will I need a rope and an ice axe?
¿Voy a necesitar una cuerda y una piqueta?

The climb is very steep.
La subida es muy escarpada.

You will need ice pitons when climbing the face.
Necesitará usted clavijas de hielo para subir por la pared.

Beware of the crevasses.
Cuidado con las grietas.

We might lose our route in the blizzard.
Puede ser que perdamos nuestra ruta en la ventisca.

You will become snow-blind if you don't use your dark glasses.
Le va a cegar el reflejo de la nieve, si no pone los lentes oscuros.

Can you let me have some cream for sunburn?
¿Me puede dejar usted la crema contra la quemadura de sol?

Did you have an easy climb yesterday?
¿Tuvo usted una subida fácil ayer?

We reached the summit at noon.
Llegamos a la cumbre al mediodía.

Can we rent pack animals here?
¿Podemos alquiler aquí las acémilas?

Is the price fixed?
¿Es un precio fijo?

Have you done any climbing?
¿Ha escalado usted antes?

The new snow is not good for climbing.
La nieve reciente no es buena para subir.

I must adjust my crampon bindings.
Tengo que ajustarme las ataduras de los crampones.

I don't like the snow; it is dangerous.
No me gusta la nieve; es peligrosa.

The snow has frozen overnight.
La nieve se ha helado durante la noche.

EMERGENCY PHRASES

There has been an accident on the mountain.
Había un accidente en la montaña.

Send for a doctor.
Mande buscar un médico.

Send for the mountain rescue team.
Mande buscar el socorro de andinismo.

What is the matter with you?
¿Qué le ocurre a usted?

I don't feel well.
No me encuentro bien.

I feel very ill.
Me siento muy mal.

I am nauseated.
Me da naúsea.

I feel weak.
Me siento débil.

He (she) is suffering from altitude sickness.
El (ella) está enfermo (enferma) de apunamiento.

He (she) must be taken to the hospital.
Hay que llevarle (llevarla) al hospital.

Is your digestion all right?
¿Está su digestíon bien?

He (she) has broken his (her) arm.
El (ella) se ha roto el brazo.

He (she) has fractured his (her) skull.
El (ella) se ha fracturado el cráneo.

You have had a bad concussion.
Ha tenido usted una conmoción seria.

I am injured.
Estoy herido.

Have you sprained your ankle?
¿Se ha torcido un tobillo?

He (she) is snow-blind.
El (ella) está ciego (ciega) del reflejo de la nieve.

Your foot is frostbitten.
Su pie está túmido.

The injured climbers were brought down on stretchers.
Bajaron en camillas los andinistas heridos.

They are lost and a rescue party set out to find them.
Los pierden y un equipo de socorro salió a buscarlos.

A mountaineer was injured (died) in a fall.
Un andinista se hirió (murió) en una caída.

We will need a stretcher.
Necesitamos una camilla.

He (she) cannot walk.
El (ella) no puede caminar.

Please help us!
¡Por favor, ayudénos!

We need help.
Necesitamos ayuda.

NOTES

1   James Ramsey Ullman, *The Age of Mountaineering* (New York, J.B. Lippincott Company, 1954), p. 139.

2   R. J. Secor, *Mexico's Volcanoes: A Climbing Guide* (Seattle, The Mountaineers Books, 1993), p. 10.

3   Johan Reinhard, "High Altitude Archeology and Andean Mountain Gods," *The American Alpine Journal,* Vol. 25, Issue 57 (1983), pp. 54-67, and Johan Reinhard, "Sacred Peaks of the Andes," *National Geographic,* Vol. 18, No. 3 (March 1992), pp. 84-111.

4   H. Adams Carter, "Ojos del Salado," *The American Alpine Journal,* Vol. 10, No. 2, Issue 31 (1957), pp. 74–96.

5   Eduardo E. Baglietto, "Determination of the Altitude of Aconcagua," *op. cit.,* pp. 91–93.

6   "New Altitude Measurements for Aconcagua and the Ojos del Salado," *The American Alpine Journal,* Vol. 32, Issue 64 (1990), pp. 202–203.

7   Alan Rouse, "Lightweight Expeditions," as quoted in Charles Clarke and Audrey Salkeld, eds., *Lightweight Expeditions to the Great Ranges* (London, The Alpine Club, 1984), p. 47.

8   Sir Martin Conway, *Aconcagua and Tierra del Fuego* (London, Cassell and Company, Ltd., 1902), pp. 97 and 107.

9   William L. Marks, "Aconcagua, Permission Problems," *The American Alpine Journal,* Vol. 23, Issue 55 (1981), pp. 236–237.

10   I celebrated the publication of the first edition of this book by embarking on an expedition to the Himalayas. I found a brand new –20-degree F sleeping bag in my duffel when I arrived at

base camp. Unbeknownst to me, my parents had removed my +20-degree F sleeping bag and replaced it with a heavier, but warmer, model. So I now use a –20-degree F sleeping bag and reflect on parental love before falling asleep. I've only zipped it all the way up once, however.

11   For those using kerosene, a primer (either alcohol or gasoline) is needed. Figure that the primer should be one-tenth of the total fuel carried. For example, a party carrying 10 liters or quarts of kerosene would need one liter of priming fluid. And for those using butane cartridges, plan on using either 80 grams or 143 milliliters of butane per person per day. And plan on packing the cartridges out! (P.S., all of these figures include an extra twenty-five percent reserve.)

12   Charles S. Houston, M.D., "Altitude Illness—Recent Advances in Knowledge," *The American Alpine Journal*, Vol. 22, No. 1 (1979), p. 155.

13   Peter H. Hackett, M.D., *Mountain Sickness: Prevention, Recognition, and Treatment* (New York, American Alpine Club, 1980), p. 60.

14   Colin Kerst Grissom, M.D., "Medical Therapy of High Altitude Illness," *The American Alpine Journal*, Vol. 35 (1993), pp. 118–123.

15   Paddy Sherman, *Expeditions to Nowhere* (Seattle, The Mountaineers, 1981), p. 184.

16   Boyd N. Everett, Jr., *The Organization of an Alaskan Expedition* (Gorak Books, Pasadena, California, 1984), pp. 84–85.

17   This literally means "terrain." *La piedra suelta* would mean a rock that is not bolted down, as opposed to what we would call a loose rock. So the use of *terreno* is correct idiomatically but not literally.

INDEX

ABOUT THE UIAA AND THE AAC

The International Mountaineering and Climbing Federation (UIAA) represents mountaineers and climbers, worldwide, on international issues. Formed in 1932, it now has over eighty-eight member associations from some seventy-six countries. Founded in 1902, the American Alpine Club (AAC) is a nonprofit organization dedicated to promoting climbing knowledge, conserving mountain environments, and serving the American climbing community.

The UIAA and AAC labels certify to the user that this publication has been endorsed by the UIAA and the AAC, that it includes a table showing the relationship between the various scales of climbing difficulty in accepted usage around the world, that its diagrams and topos are compatible with the mapping symbols in common usage, that it contains sketch maps of the area and accident and rescue information, and that it contains a summary of any access or environmental problems. No other certification or warranty is intended or may be implied.

By affixing the UIAA and AAC labels to this publication, the UIAA and AAC assume no responsibility for and expressly do not warrant the accuracy of any information contained herein. This includes, but is not limited to, maps, route descriptions, and rescue information.

Rock climbing, ice climbing, ski mountaineering, and mountaineering are inherently dangerous activities. The UIAA and AAC do not recommend that

anyone participate in these activities unless they are experts, seek qualified instruction or guidance, are knowledgeable about the risks involved, and are willing to assume responsibility for those risks.

The UIAA General Assembly has resolved to adopt the following principles and guidelines as a program for concrete action:

The Kathmandu Declaration on Mountain Activities

1. There is an urgent need for effective protection of the mountain environment and landscape.
2. The flora, fauna, and natural resources of all kinds need immediate attention, care, and concern.
3. Actions designed to reduce the negative impact of man's activities on mountains should be encouraged.
4. The cultural heritage and the dignity of the local population are inviolable.
5. All activities designed to restore and rehabilitate the mountain world need to be encouraged.
6. Contacts between mountaineers of different regions and countries should be increasingly encouraged in the spirit of friendship, mutual respect, and peace.
7. Information and education for improving the relationship between man and his environment should be available for wider and wider sections of society.
8. The use of appropriate technology for energy needs and the proper disposal of waste in mountain areas are matters of immediate concern.
9. There is need for more international support—governmental as well as nongovernmental—to the developing mountain countries, for instance, in matters of ecological conservation.
10. The need for widening access to mountain areas in order to promote their appreciation and study should be unfettered by political considerations.

Kathmandu, October 1982

INTERNATIONAL GRADING TABLE

Australia	France	Germany (UIAA)	South Africa	UK		USA* *Yosemite decimal system
	1	i		VD	3	
	2	ii				
13	3	iii		MS	4	5.6
14	4	iv	13	S		5.7
15	4+		14			
			15	VS	5a	5.8
		v	16			
16	5		17			5.9
17	5+	vi–	18	HVS	5b	5.10a
			19	E1		5.10b
18	6a	vi	20			5.10c
19	6a+	vi+		E2		5.10d
20	6b	vii–	21		5c	5.11a
21	6b+	vii	22	E3		5.11b
22	6c	vii+	23			5.11c
23	6c+	viii–	24	E4	6a	5.11d
24	7a	viii	25			5.12a
25	7a+	viii+	26	E5		5.12b
	7b					5.12c
26	7b+	ix–	27		6b	5.12c
27	7c	ix	28	E6		5.12d
28	7c+		29			5.13a
29	8a	ix+	30	E7	6c	5.13b
30	8a+	x–	31			5.13c
31	8b	x	32	E8		5.13d
32	8b+	x+	33			5.14a
33	8c	xi–		E9		5.14b
34	8c+				7a	5.14c
		xi			7b	
	9a	xi+		E10		5.14d